"The Scriptures are filled with images of a God who is casting down the mighty and lifting up the lowly, of the last becoming first and the first last. In relentless nonconformity to the patterns of our culture, the Christian call is not to move away from suffering but to move toward it, so that we can bear some of the burdens carried by our brothers and sisters. Here is one story of the downward mobility of the Kingdom. It is a story that dares you to move closer to the margins, to the suffering, to the pain…and to meet Jesus there—in His many disguises."

—SHANE CLAIBORNE, best-selling author, activist, and
recovering sinner

"Under the Overpass is a captivating, terrifying, encouraging, motivating, saddening, amazing account of a young man who died to self with the assurance that God knows best. Rarely does a book move me this much. Mike Yankoski doesn't have a little liquid fire in his heart; he is consumed by it. Let his book ignite your heart and soul."

—RYAN DOBSON, best-selling author of *Be Intolerant* and
To Die For

"Every once in a while a book comes along that is so raw and revealing it proves to be a catalyst for cognizance and conviction for multiple generations. Under the Overpass is such a book. Mike and Sam's five-month journey through the underbelly of America was not a brazen stunt by bored college students but a quest born out of guilt and curiosity that became a Christ-fueled passion for the poor and dispossessed. I know Mike and am inspired by the fact that his zeal has intensified over time. He lives what he learned on the streets. Be careful as you read this timely book; it could radically change your perceptions and maybe even your calling."

—JOHN ASHMEN, president, Association of Gospel
 Rescue Missions

"Often it's hard to understand why God calls us to do difficult things. But when we're willing to answer His call, our lives are forever changed. Mike and Sam were willing to say, 'Here I am, Lord,' and I have no doubt that their story will change you too!"

—BRAD MEULI, president, Denver Rescue Mission

"Everyone with a beating heart will benefit from reading this book. Leading through example, Mike Yankoski takes readers on his amazing journey through the forgotten streets of America. Into the darkest places where most choose not to look, Mike chose to go. This book is so deeply moving that emotion is soon overrun with an honest desire to make a difference for what our dear Lord calls 'the least of these.'"

—KIM MEEDER, best-selling author of *Hope Rising*

UNDER THE OVERPASS

FOREWORD BY FRANCIS CHAN

UNDER THE
OVERPASS

A JOURNEY OF FAITH
ON THE STREETS
OF AMERICA

MIKE YANKOSKI

UPDATED AND EXPANDED EDITION

MULTNOMAH
BOOKS

UNDER THE OVERPASS
MULTNOMAH BOOKS
12265 Oracle Boulevard, Suite 200
Colorado Springs, Colorado 80921

Scripture quotations are taken from the Holy Bible, New International Version®. NIV®. Copyright © 1973, 1978, 1984 by Biblica Inc.™ Used by permission of Zondervan. All rights reserved worldwide. www.zondervan.com.

Details in some anecdotes and stories have been changed to protect the identities of the persons involved.

ISBN 978-1-59052-402-2
ISBN 978-0-307-56343-9 (electronic)

Published in the United States by WaterBrook Multnomah, an imprint of the Crown Publishing Group, a division of Random House Inc., New York.

MULTNOMAH and its mountain colophon are registered trademarks of Random House Inc.

Library of Congress Cataloging-in-Publication Data
Yankoski, Michael.
    Under the overpass / by Michael Yankoski.
       p. cm.
    ISBN 978-1-59052-402-2
  1. Yankoski, Michael. 2. Homeless persons—United States—Biography. 3.
Homelessness—United States—Anecdotes. 4. Homelessness—United States—Case
studies. I. Title.
    HV4505.Y36 2005
    305.5'692'092—dc22

                                                           2004027331

Printed in the United States of America
2012

10 9 8 7 6 5 4 3 2

SPECIAL SALES
Most WaterBrook Multnomah books are available at special quantity discounts when purchased in bulk by corporations, organizations, and special-interest groups. Custom imprinting or excerpting can also be done to fit special needs. For information, please e-mail SpecialMarkets@WaterBrookMultnomah.com or call 1-800-603-7051.

CONTENTS

viii

FOREWORD
TO THE UPDATED AND EXPANDED EDITION

by Francis Chan

would like to write a few words about Mike Yankoski, and then I'll give some thoughts about his book... I am a very skeptical person, and I struggle with cynicism. Like most people, I have heard so many lies that now I have a hard time trusting. I even struggle when reading a good book, because in the back of my mind I'm wondering if the person who wrote it is for real.

So what is it about Mike that inclines me to trust him? The sacrifices he has made.

Sacrifice promotes believability.

The apostle Paul defended his ministry in 2 Corinthians 11 with a list of hardships he endured. It was his suffering for the sake of the gospel that gave credence to his message. Paul showed that he genuinely believed what he taught. Why else would he suffer as he did? His argument in 1 Corinthians 15 is similar as he explains the foolishness of his lifestyle if the gospel isn't true.

While there are many who say they live for eternity, Mike and his wife, Danae, are among the few I actually believe. Their actions have shown me that I can trust them. You can too.

Now about the book…

I was warned when entering seminary that if I was not careful, a dangerous habit could form: I could learn to read the Bible and *do* nothing in response. I still remember our seminary president warning us that study to the neglect of action becomes easier and easier with each occurrence. We should be terrified if we have mastered the art of becoming convicted and doing nothing in response. Don't read Mike's book if you're not willing to change your attitude and actions toward the homeless.

As a person who considers himself sensitive to the needs of the rejected in our country, I learned from this book that I still have a ways to go. I look forward to seeing the changes God will bring about in my life because of it.

Mike shows much grace in pointing out weaknesses our churches may have in caring for the poor. It is embarrassing to admit, but I have often struggled with pride when encountering the homeless. I can't say that I usually see them as having equal worth with me, much less consider them as "better" than myself (Philippians 2:3). Like many, I have found myself at times working to avoid rather than seeking to engage.

Far from condemning, this book actually causes me to look forward to my next encounter with those living on the streets. I believe it will do the same for you. As I followed Mike's journey and tried to put myself in his shoes, it caused me to love Jesus more. As I thought of what a struggle it would be for me to leave my comforts, it stirred a greater adoration toward my Savior, who emptied Himself to dwell with us.

This is how we know what love is: Jesus Christ laid down his life for us. And we ought to lay down our lives for our brothers. If anyone has material possessions and sees his brother in need but has no pity on him, how can the love of God be in him? Dear children, let us not love with words or tongue but with actions and in truth. (1 John 3:16–18)

I pray that the story of Mike and Sam's five-month journey causes you to eagerly anticipate your next encounter with a homeless man or woman, created in the image of God.

—FRANCIS CHAN

xi

NOTE TO THE READER

Before you take the first step on this journey, I need to tell you something. Common street lingo isn't pretty. People can pack more expletives and profanities into one sentence than you'd think possible. Vulgarities and crude insults become part of everyday conversation, even between friends. But out of respect for our readers and the standards of this publisher, this element of street life is not present in the pages you're about to read.

TWENTY MINUTES PAST THE WORLD

Real punches aren't as sharp and clean as Hollywood makes them out to be. They're much deeper, thicker. If you happen to hear them from close-up, the sound doesn't give you a rush of adrenaline. It makes your stomach sink.

The punches, screams, cursing, and kicking we witnessed that night in the park were real. The blood was real, too. It was another cold night in San Francisco...

PAYBACK

I had walked against the wind over to where Sam was sitting, his back up to the concrete and brick wall that circles the planter at the Haight Street entrance to Golden Gate Park. All I'd had to eat that day was a ninety-nine-cent hamburger, and it sat uncomfortably in my stomach. I groaned, stretched, and sat down next to Sam, rubbing my hands together to try to get some feeling back in my fingers.

"You know you're cold when your fingers are too stiff to play the guitar," Sam said.

He had laid his guitar carefully across some dead flowers in the planter behind us. Fog billowed high above us, and every now and then, a cold gust pushed trash and dust into our faces. The air was rank with the stench of alcohol, cigarettes, body odor, and joints. Even with the wind it was sickening.

Nearby, six street people played quarters, a game in which the person throwing a quarter closest to the wall but not touching it took everyone else's quarters. It was a good way to pass the time and make a little cash.

One of the girls threw a quarter that clanked sharply against the wall. A horrible throw. She let out a string of curses, then ambled over to a heavily tattooed guy leaning against a cast iron fence and smoking a joint. She kissed him, not seeming to notice that she was interrupting his conversation with the man next to him.

"Can I have a quarter, baby?" she pleaded, looking into his eyes.

"Sure," he growled. He reached into his pocket and pulled out two dirty quarters.

The girl snatched them and ran back to the game, ready for the next round.

"You'll pay me back later," he yelled after her.

"You bet I will," the girl said with a wry smile in his direction.

A fresh gust of wet wind pushed me further into my filthy sweatshirt. San Francisco cold is weird—heavy and penetrating. Two months earlier on the streets of Washington, D.C., Sam and I couldn't do enough to escape the heat.

Sam was talking. "There is this mountain back home we used to hike up early in the mornings just to watch the sunrise. One time we wanted to play worship music up there, so we carried a guitar all the way to the top. But when we got there, no one could play it because we were all so cold."

Sam looked deeper into Golden Gate Park, stretching away from us for two miles to the Pacific Ocean. "Man. Seems like such a long time ago."

"Yep, sure does," I said, my own thoughts turning back to take comfort in familiar wonderings: My family would probably be sitting down to eat dinner together, while my friends back at school might be heading out to watch a movie.

"It sure does," I said again.

That's when the chaos hit.

"Who you think you are? You piece of...!" Marco, the undisputed leader of the gang at the mouth of the park, was screaming at a guy in front of him. Then with all eyes on him, Marco slammed both fists into the guy's chest, forcing all the air out of the man with a sickening whoosh and knocking him down.

Instantly the park erupted with screams and profanity as everyone seemingly rushed to join the fight. The coin tossers next to us ran to join in, too, the last throw spinning unheeded until it clinked to a stop.

Within seconds, about twenty guys were throwing punches, kicking, yelling, cursing, and tearing wildly at each other. Dogs barked and snarled. And thirty or so other park people, many of them drunk and staggering, gathered around to cheer.

In the center of it all, Marco was pulling on one end of his victim while the man's friends were pulling from the other. Allies of Marco saw their opportunity and set about to pound the defenseless man's face or plant steel-toed boots in his gut.

When blood started dripping onto the cement, the brawl seemed to get more feverish. "Take him in! Take him in!"

3

someone yelled. They wanted to drag their prey deeper into the park, away from the cops or any passerby who might try to spoil their fun.

By now, Sam and I were standing, looking around for a squad car—for any sign that this wouldn't end with a dead man in Golden Gate Park. Nothing.

"We probably need to get out of here," I mumbled. Sam agreed.

As we picked up our stuff and shuffled off, the brawl shifted further into the park. All I could think to do was pray—and wonder again what Sam and I had been thinking when we decided to step out of our comfortable world...and into this.

A FLICKER OF LIGHTNING

The idea had dropped into my brain one Sunday morning while I sat in church. The pastor was delivering a powerful sermon about living the Christian life. The gist of it was, "Be the Christian you say you are."

Suddenly I was shocked to realize that I had just driven twenty minutes past the world that needed me to be the Christian I say I am, in order to hear a sermon entitled "Be the Christian you say you are." Soon I would drive back past that same world to the privilege of my comfortable life on campus at a Christian college.

Thinking ahead to my next week, I knew several things would happen. I knew I'd hear more lectures about being a caring Christian or living a godly life. I'd read more books about who God is and about what the world needs now. I'd spend more time late at night down at a coffee shop with my friends kicking around ultimate questions and finely delivered opinions about the world.

Then I'd jump into my warm bed and turn out the light. Another day gone.

But we were created to be and to do, not merely to discuss. The hypocrisy in my life troubled me. No, I wasn't in the grip of rampant sin, but at the same time, for the life of me I couldn't find a connecting thread of radical, living obedience between what I *said* about my world and how I *lived* in it. Sure, I claimed that Christ was my stronghold, my peace, my sustenance, my joy. But I did all that from the safety of my comfortable upper-middle-class life. I never really had to put my claims to the test.

I sat there in church struggling to remember a time when I'd actually needed to lean fully on Christ rather than on my own abilities. Not much came to mind. What was Paul's statement in Philippians? "I have learned what it means to be content in all circumstances, whether with everything or with nothing" (Philippians 4:11–12).

With nothing?

The idea came instantly—like the flash of a camera or a flicker of lightning. It left me breathless, and it changed my life. *What if I stepped out of my comfortable life with nothing but God and put my faith to the test alongside of those who live with nothing every day?*

The picture that came with that question was of me homeless and hungry on the streets of an American city.

Hard on the heels of the idea came the questions: What if I didn't actually believe the things I argued with so much certainty? What, for example, if I didn't truly believe that Christ is my identity, my strength, my hope? Or worse, what

5

if I leaped in faith, but God didn't catch me? My mind reeled.

And then there were the practical questions. Could I survive on the streets? How much did I really want to learn to be content *always* with *nothing*? What would my friends think? What would my parents think? My pastors? My professors? Would I be okay? What if I got sick? What if I starved? What if I got beat up? What if I froze?

What if I'm wrong?

Am I crazy?

Will I die?

But already, I had decided. I walked out of church that morning seized by a big idea, assaulted by dozens of questions, and sure that I had heard deep in my heart a still, small voice saying, "Follow Me."

6

"WHY WOULD YOU WANT TO DO *THAT?*"

Of course, what my idea might actually require took a while to sink in. I would have to put the rest of my life on hold, leave school, and sign up for months of risk, rejection, and plain old misery. There aren't too many brochures for that kind of thing.

I started with my family. When I called to give them my long, excited ramble, I heard only silence on the other end. Then a few expressions of stunned disbelief.

"Why would you want to do *that?*" my dad asked.

Determined to hear him out, I asked him to explain what he meant.

He did. "Why would you want to leave school, leave your friends, leave your family, leave your life, and do this? Why would you put your mother and me through the stress, confusion, and worry? Why would you jeopardize all that you've worked so hard for, all that we've paid for, all that you have to look forward to—for *this?*"

Each of his questions hit home. I thought for a moment. "Well," I said finally, "that's sort of complicated. I believe I must. I don't know for certain yet that I will do this, I still have a lot of people to talk with. But I believe that it is something I must do."

I would be heading home for the summer in a couple of months at which time my parents said we could discuss this crazy idea a little more. We agreed to talk about it face-to-face. It would be a hard conversation.

I plunged into researching homelessness on the streets of America. I read firsthand accounts, sociological studies, autobiographies of people who had given their lives to work with the homeless and addicted.

Even at first glance, the scope of homelessness in America was much worse than I'd imagined. According to the National Coalition for the Homeless, in the United States, more than 3.5 million people experience homelessness during any given year. That means that more than one percent of our population this year will be eating out of trash cans and sleeping under bridges.

Soon I was meeting every month with the director of the Santa Barbara Rescue Mission. Then I began volunteering at the mission twice a week to learn more about the men and women who came through its doors.

Over the next year, I probably looked like any other college student—studying hard, playing hard, juggling classes and work. But all the while I kept pushing on my crazy idea. To my surprise, at every turn and with every conversation, the idea was only confirmed. Even people who should have been telling me no encouraged me to press on.

THE COUNSEL OF FRIENDS

One day I sat in the office of the president of the Denver Rescue Mission, laying out my thoughts. I figured if anyone would know enough to tell me to turn back, he'd be the one. But after he thought for a while, he looked up at me, puzzled by what he was about to say.

"I can't believe I'm saying this," he said, "but I think your idea is a good one. And I have a feeling that it is very important for you to do this. It will be dangerous, of course, and there are no guarantees. But if you plan well, you can succeed. And you certainly won't come back the same person."

I walked out of his office convinced for the first time that what I wanted to happen actually *would* happen. And something else—an invitation to begin my journey by checking in to his facility just like any other transient off the street.

About this time I also became convinced that I needed some kind of advisory group that would give me guidance and hold me accountable. Proverbs 15:22 says, "Plans fail for lack of counsel, but with many advisers they succeed." I wanted to be wise, and to succeed, and more than that, I wanted to bring glory to the Lord in everything this idea entailed. So I began praying that God would lead me to the right men.

It didn't take long to develop a list of men who had been, and still were, having a significant impact on my life as a Christian: my campus pastor, my youth pastor, two rescue mission presidents, a close friend from Oregon, and a professor. Each man I talked to responded positively to my proposal and agreed to mentor and advise me.

With their help, I began putting a travel plan together. After considering a lot of alternatives, we settled on six cities: Denver; Washington, D.C.; Portland; San Francisco; Phoenix; and San Diego. These cities seemed representative of the American urban homeless scene as well as being places where I would have a backup personal contact of some kind in case of emergency.

My advisers also helped me fine-tune my overall purpose. We boiled it down to three objectives:

1. To better understand the life of the homeless in America, and to see firsthand how the church is responding to their needs.
2. To encourage others to "live out loud" for Christ in whatever ways God is asking them to.
3. To learn personally what it means to depend on Christ for my daily physical needs, and to experience contentment and confidence in Him.

ENTER SAM

Then there was the issue of companionship. Jesus sent His disciples out two-by-two—a model that seemed right for my new undertaking as well. Besides, I *wanted* a traveling partner. I pictured long, lonely nights huddled in a stairwell. I worried about attacks. Another person would make everything easier.

But a traveling partner turned out to be hard to come by.

Some friends I approached didn't catch the vision. Others couldn't take time off from school or work. Three months before I was to depart on the streets, it looked as though I would be going alone. And then I met Sam Purvis.

At six-foot-three or so, Sam was big—about the same size as me, which was an added bonus. Two big guys are much less likely to get messed with on the streets. He was easygoing and he needed a haircut. Right away, I saw possibilities.

Sam had gone to the University of Oklahoma for a semester but was taking a semester off. He happened to be on my campus, and heard through the grapevine about my proposed journey. The more we talked, the more interested he became in joining me. I was encouraged by Sam's excitement about the trip and passion for serving the Lord. Although we only had a few conversations, I felt a real connection and unity in our hearts and vision.

We agreed to take two weeks to think and pray about it, and for Sam to meet with his mentor and pastor back in his Oregon hometown. Two Saturdays later, during a two-hour telephone conversation, Sam and I struck a deal.

TRAVELING PAPERS

Sam and I decided we would be gone for five months. We would begin at the rescue mission in Denver, then travel to and live on the streets of Washington, D.C.; Portland; San Francisco; Phoenix; and San Diego.

From the start, Sam and I understood that we would not actually *be* homeless. We'd only be travelers through this underworld of need—privileged visitors, really, because any time we wished, we could leave the streets and come home.

Most people on the streets have no such option.

Yet, as truly as we could, Sam and I wanted to *experience* homelessness. That meant, among other things, that we'd carry only the bare essentials, taking no cell phones, credit cards, or extra clothes. We would survive as most other men and women on the streets do—panhandling for money, eating at rescue missions or out of garbage cans, and sleeping outside or in shelters.

We would take only what we could carry. Our clothing for the five months would consist of a pair of boxers, a pair of shorts, a pair of jeans, a T-shirt, and a sweatshirt. Add books and journals, and a couple of battered guitars to support our panhandling, and that was it.

We would keep our background and purpose a secret because if a person or an organization knew we were *choosing* to be homeless, their response to us would be different. As much as possible, we wanted to experience the real thing.

We'd travel by Greyhound Bus, using our panhandling earnings to buy fare between cities. But because we wanted to spend our time homeless in the cities rather than stuck on a bus for two weeks crossing the country, we made two exceptions: we would fly between Denver and Washington, D.C., and between D.C. and Portland.

To stay in contact with our families, our advisers, and those who were praying for us, we'd use e-mail at local libraries plus an occasional phone call. In case one of us got stabbed or needed to make an immediate trip to the hospital, we took enough cash for a one-way cab ride, praying we wouldn't ever use it (we didn't).

That left two major purchases for our new life on the streets. A few days before we left, Sam I went down to a local

11

thrift store and bought two sleeping bags (at three dollars apiece) and two backpacks (at four dollars).

Seven dollars each.

We were ready.

INVITATION TO THE JOURNEY

On May 27 we stepped out of our old lives. From then until November 2, Sam and I slept out in the open or in shelters or under bridges. We ate out of trash cans and feeding kitchens. We looked disgusting, smelled disgusting, were disgusting. We were shunned and forgotten and ignored by most people who walked past us—good, acceptable people who looked just like Sam and I used to look, and maybe just like you.

Although our journey took us to many destinations that were challenging, cold, and even brutal—like the night in Golden Gate Park—by God's grace we did what we set out to do, and learned a lot along the way. For example: that faith is much more than just an "amen" at the end of the sermon on Sunday mornings; that the comfort and security we strive so hard to create for ourselves doesn't even come close to the "life in the full" that Christ promises; and that God is faithful and good, even when we're not.

Perhaps you, too, have felt a nudging toward a life on the edge—some place or task in your life where, as Frederick Buechner put it, "God's great mercy and the world's great hunger meet." If you haven't yet, is your heart open to that moment when it comes?

Either way, I invite you to take this journey with Sam and me through the everyday world of the hundreds of thousands of men, women, and children who make up America's homeless population. We decided to go past the edge with God. One day soon, I pray you will, too. And when you do, I think you'll find what we did…

A bigger world, and more reason to care for it.

More forgotten, ruined, beautiful people than we ever imagined existed, and more reason to hope in their redemption.

A greater God, and more reason to journey with Him anywhere.

DENVER

"The best way to find out if we had second-class citizens and what their plight was, would be to become one of them."

JOHN HOWARD GRIFFIN, *BLACK LIKE ME*

Start: May 27th, 2003
End: June 27th, 2003
Duration: 31 days
Location: Mike: Lawrence Street Mission
Sam: The Farm, another D.R.M. rehab facility

We decided early in our planning period that we'd benefit from some help making the changeover from campus to street life. So, at the suggestion of our advisers, Sam and I decided to make Denver a transition time from one world to the other.

We went to the Denver Rescue Mission. By being "members" of the live-in drug rehab program, Sam and I could live with men very similar to the homeless on the streets, but in a more protected environment. We were less likely to get stabbed in a place where knives weren't allowed than on the streets where rules don't really exist.

The transition made everyone—family, friends, advisers, and Sam and me—more at ease. But it turned out to be a good plan for other reasons, too. Sam and I had a lot to learn. The streets come with different lifestyles, different assumptions, different habits, different risks.

The days in the rescue mission allowed us some time to adjust, to prepare for the months ahead, and to let a new set of survival instincts kick in.

A LONG WAY FROM HOME

Gently, no, regretfully I shut the door of my father's car. We were about two blocks from the Denver Rescue Mission, the place where I would be staying amidst fifty recovering drug addicts and 150 homeless wanderers for the next thirty days.

I remembered a time or two having my dad drop me a block away from a friend's house, or school, or the movies when I was younger in order to avoid being seen with him. Somehow it had made me feel older, stronger, more independent. Today's separation made me feel young and weak. Part of me desperately wished that I were venturing toward such a safe, familiar place on this scorching afternoon, instead of delving into a world I knew little about.

With a last wave I turned and walked slowly away, my steps sounding muffled on the hot concrete as Dad drove away. For this part of our sojourn, Sam and I were actually going separate ways. Sam would spend his time at another rescue mission rehab facility north of the city.

In seconds, I was sweating. The traffic consisted of mostly old run-down clunkers to fit this old, run-down clunky neighborhood. Every doubt I could think of screamed in my head.

What's a yuppie college kid from California doing on these streets with the drug addicts and ex-cons?

Psalm 118:6 ran through my mind. *The Lord is with me; I will not be afraid. What can man do to me?* So, would God be with me? And if He was, would that be enough to quiet my fears? I would soon find out. I breathed a prayer for Sam and forced myself to keep putting one foot in front of the other until I stood looking up at the front door of the mission.

It towered ominously over me. I paused. "Not exactly friendly," I muttered to myself, then stepped up and swung it open.

I entered a big lobby furnished with only a desk and a water cooler. The man at the desk popped his gum. "Help you?" he asked.

A ceiling fan whirred silently above him, but it didn't seem to be moving any air.

17

"I'm here to enter the program," I said, shifting my pack. "A friend said it would be good to come here."

Thus began the process every new rehab program member has to go through—I had an interview with an intake chaplain. All day every day this man dealt with hardcore drug addicts. Today, on a hot May afternoon, he was talking to a twenty-year-old kid with long hair and a white T-shirt who looked more like he had stumbled out of the 70s than a drug addiction. And I wanted into his mission.

I wasn't about to lie, wasn't going to pretend that I was an addict or a felon. That left me pretty unsure of how I would convince this man to let me stay at the mission without telling him everything about our homeless endeavor. I explained to him that there were a lot of things I needed to figure out and mentioned that a friend had told me I should come to the mission. Although entirely true, it was vague, but for reasons of safety and authenticity, I knew I needed to keep my real identity to myself. (Only the mission president knew the full story.)

I guess the heat of the afternoon helped, because after I had finished being vague, the chaplain got right to the point. "You're not going to be like most of the other guys here in the mission. You realize that, don't you?"

"Yeah. I know," I answered, feeling awkward.

"But..." he continued, "if you *want* to be here, and aren't going to cause us any problems, then we're happy to have you." Then he walked over to shake my hand.

As we walked out into the lobby, the chaplain told me that a lot of guys moved in and out of the mission on a daily basis. "They relapse and start using again," he said, "and we have to expel them for a month. It's policy. We actually had two guys leave this morning."

I filled out some general forms, checked the no boxes next to the questions about felonies, convictions, and parole, took a short tour of the facilities, got assigned a bed and a locker, and finished up with a run through the supply room to get soap, shampoo, a toothbrush and toothpaste. Within an hour I was officially part of the program.

Up in the bunk hall, I walked past row after row of beds, some nicely made up with clean sheets, others just bare, stained mattresses. Each night every bed in the mission would be filled with a snoring body, either a member of the rehab program or one of the homeless men who ate dinner and was on rotation for a bed that night.

I'd been assigned a bottom bunk with a sagging mattress

18

and a single, narrow locker with chipped paint and a lock that didn't really work. I thought of all the things I usually considered my essentials: car, laptop, music, mountain bike, clothes. Not much of it would fit in here! Thoreau says "simplify, simplify, simplify," but at that moment I couldn't help wondering if I had gone too far.

But I was exhausted from the stress of the afternoon, so I pulled my sheets over the mattress and stretched out. My weight made the springs creak and complain.

I was staring up at the ancient springs above me, just about to fall asleep, when a man came in and threw himself down on the next bunk.

"Hey, neighbor!" he said, happy for someone new to talk with. "How are you doin'? Comin' down off of anything?"

I shook my head, and we introduced ourselves. His name was Taylor. My first friend on the road. He wore jeans, a blue shirt, and tennis shoes that looked a little too small for his feet—standard, donated, mission-approved rehab wear. Taylor's shirt was actually in better shape than some of the others I'd seen, and he soon explained why. He had a new job in the clothing room. Every night the mission provided clothes to any of the homeless who had come in for dinner, but rehab members got first pick since they had to do the sorting. Taylor had already added significantly to his wardrobe.

An alcoholic and methamphetamine addict, Taylor had been living at the mission since early spring. At that point, he explained, his life was a wreck. He had nowhere to go and was ready to end his life. But the mission had done incredible things for him. He said he still craved drugs but could now say no to them as he had never been able to do before.

"This place isn't so bad" he said, kicking back. "You can hear the fans at the Rockies games cheering through this window right here. And the work could be worse. Just make sure you don't get caught slacking off. That really pisses people off around here. They call it work therapy, and well, they *really* want you to get better!"

Work therapy was the mission's method of teaching basic life skills to men who had long ago dropped out of any kind of structured existence. Food deliveries had to be carried from the street down to basement storage rooms every day. The mission had to be swept and mopped constantly. Men got trash detail, or were assigned to the mission warehouse/sorting facility, or to various other tasks. Even personal hygiene was considered work therapy, and everyone was required to shower and shave daily.

20

Every rehab member was also required to listen for the mission-wide intercom that announced the arrival of deliveries at the front door. When the voice came, we all had to stop what we were doing and pitch in. Deliveries might be fresh doughnuts, produce, milk, clothes, furniture, shoes, or other items of value. But every now and then, because donors could get tax write-offs, we'd be hauling in worthless junk or rotten food.

I never really got that nap I was so close to before Taylor showed up. My first afternoon I carried down boxes of rotting fruit and crates of moldy bread, each of which we threw directly into the dumpsters. The mission did everything possible to serve healthy, hearty meals to its clients. Just because some homeless folks eat out of dumpsters doesn't mean a mission should serve up garbage for dinner.

By six o'clock, we were worn out from hauling deliveries, and when the voice came on announcing dinner, several of the guys let out a cheer and we all headed to the basement where the cafeteria was located.

Dinner was, well, not what I was used to. As I was pouring myself a glass of milk, I noticed that the milk had expired ten days earlier. Remembering the rotten fruit and bread we had already thrown out, I paused, wondering what would happen if I drank the milk. Luckily another member of the rehab program called to me from the food line. I set the glass of milk down and walked over to him, grateful for an excuse to leave it on the table.

The main course was a vegetable and meat goulash. I asked for a lot of salad. Halfway through the meal, though, one of the other rehab guys walked over to the table that had the milk on it and loudly noticed that someone had poured him a glass. Picking up the cup he downed the whole glass and then poured himself another from the expired container before walking back to his table. That left me feeling foolish—and aware that I hadn't a clue what hunger and living without meant yet. To set things right, I picked up my fork and dug into the goulash. It wasn't too bad. (A lot of my assumptions would be falling away during that month.)

After dinner was over and we had cleaned up the cafeteria, I climbed back up the four flights of stairs to the dorm room, exhausted. A sagging mattress had never sounded so good.

That night I lay in my bed, a hundred and fifty other men snoring around me. A halogen streetlight shone weakly through the dirty windows and bathed the room in pale blue.

Lying there, in the same room as 150 drug addicts, felons, alcoholics, and homeless men, with Taylor snoring not three feet away, I suddenly felt entirely weak, unable, and inadequate to bridge the gap between myself and these men. Then

21

I realized I didn't have to bridge that chasm. That wasn't my responsibility. My responsibility was simply to be there, and to trust that the Lord would use me, that He would bridge the distance.

Paul's encouragement to young Timothy came to mind—that God didn't give us a spirit of fearfulness but "a spirit of power, of love and of self-discipline" (2 Timothy 1:7).

I prayed for more of that spirit, rolled over, and went to sleep.

COLD TURKEY

The next few days taught me just how much the mission staff "wanted me to get better," as Taylor had put it. The work was intense. Every rehab member, in addition to doing whatever the voice on the intercom asked, was assigned work each day. These were posted the night before. We'd all crowd around the list like high school guys pressing against a football roster. If you got dish duty, you walked away relieved. If you had to scrub toilets, you walked away groaning.

The first couple of days I swept and mopped the hallways or the bunk hall, which was a great time to get to know the other guys assigned to the same job. We would orchestrate our broom pushing across the linoleum so we could talk.

Alley duty had to be the worst job. A narrow alley at the back of the mission separated it from an abandoned warehouse. Back there the mission kept four dumpsters where we threw the rotting food that was donated. The homeless also used the dumpsters as outhouses. In the midday heat of summer, a brutal stench hung over that alley. Those on alley duty were given thick rubber gloves, rubber boots, a face mask, a power washer, and a gallon of bleach and told to "have a go at it."

At least suffering can draw people together. I worked two hours a day for four days on alley duty with Roy and James. We breathed through our mouths as we sprayed, trying to keep the stench from beating us back, so talk was limited. It seemed like no matter how much we scrubbed or how much bleach we poured out, we just couldn't win. Each day when we came out again, the alley and the dumpsters reeked just as unbelievably as they had the previous morning. We were ready to give up in disgust when the roster changed, and we got different duties.

- - -

My life at the mission rather quickly fell into a routine. Every day after we ate in the downstairs cafeteria, the newest rehab members had to stay after and help out with meals for the homeless. A couple of guys would hand out trays full of food, while a few more picked up the empty trays and wiped down the spot for the next person. Still others made sure the trash didn't get too full, and then a whole crew helped make the line of hungry people run smoothly.

I stood taking in the scene from a corner of the cafeteria one evening, a week after I had entered the mission. More than one hundred homeless men and women were in the room, and a line of another 150 stretched out the door and up the stairs. All that suffering and brokenness in one place was difficult to watch at first, and the smell was hard to bear. So many lives in such a difficult state, so much sweat, so much dirt, so much decay. Earlier that same day I had spilled some spaghetti sauce on my own shirt and, frustrated, went to the bathroom to scrub out the stain. But I felt foolish as a filthy man limped past me. His once white T-shirt was now almost black.

I watched an old man take a slow, thankful sip of coffee and put his cup back on the table, careful not to spill a drop. "Come all you who are weary...," said Jesus. It was moving to watch the weary man come, even more to see his desperation give way to peace, if only for a little while. His hair was long, gray, and knotted at nearly every strand and his beard, though not as long as his hair, was speckled here and there with bits of food that had missed their mark.

I walked over to get the tray off a table in front of another man. He was haggard but had a kind face. When he caught me smiling at him, he sat up straight. "A smile is such an easy thing to give away, don't you think?" he asked. A goofy grin spread across his face, showing some remains of his dinner and proving he didn't own a single tooth.

I couldn't help laughing. "You've given away quite a few, haven't you?" I said, working over the table.

"That I have, son," he said with a wink. His name was Peter. "I was a clown for a long time," he told me as I continued cleaning. "Some people didn't like me much, so they knocked out my teeth here and there."

"Ouch!" I said, not really knowing how else to respond.

Peter shrugged, and slurped coffee across his bare gums. Then he changed the subject. "How do you like the rehab program here?"

"It's great," I said. "A lot of people here seem to be getting their lives back together."

24

"I think I'm going to try and get in here." He looked determined. "I've been on the streets too long, been addicted too long, been dying too long. Do you think it'll work?"

I sat down facing him. "You mean do I think you can get over your addiction and get on with your life?" I asked.

Peter thought a minute. "Yeah, that's what I mean," he said.

"Well, I'm sure it won't be easy, but yes, I do think you can graduate from this program. Do you want it bad enough?"

Peter nodded slowly. "Yeah, I want it bad enough. The streets are too hard."

- - -

The next day Peter entered the mission early in the afternoon, going through the same process I had the week earlier. He was assigned a bed a few rows down from me and seemed to be settling in fine, thankful for a space to call his own, a roof over his head, and three meals a day.

Men entering the mission were required to stop using whatever drugs they might be on. Cold turkey. For many, this meant an intense, painful detox period during which their bodies were learning to live without their chemical dependencies. The agony was almost unbearable just to watch.

A few days after we met, I walked past Peter's bed. He was under the covers even though it was a ninety-degree day. His entire face was contorted with agony, and he shook uncontrollably, legs jerking and kicking as he thrashed about. Sweat beaded across his forehead and ran down his neck, and his hair was dripping wet.

Alarmed, I knelt beside his bunk, yelling to ask him if

he was okay, if there was anything I could do. But he gave no sign that he heard me. He just stared wildly, unseeing, unable to speak.

Another rehab member walked past and stopped, only casually interested.

"Man, he's coming down hard," he said, looking at Peter's contortions. "Lifetime addict."

I asked him if there was anything we could do.

"Naw. He'll be alright," the guy said. "Just let him come down. It hurts, but he'll be okay. He'll wish he'd never even *started* using—but that can be a good thing."

Peter didn't leave his bed for two days. He told me later that he didn't remember me kneeling by his bed, or yelling at him. On the third day, though, Peter showed up for breakfast in the cafeteria, looking utterly exhausted, like he had just fought and lost the biggest battle of his life. But he had won.

Several men voiced their support when he walked in, and intermittent nods around the room during the meal affirmed for Peter that others understood and were glad he'd made it. They'd all gone through hell, but had, by the Lord's grace, come out ready to change.

Peter grabbed his tray of food and set it down on the table next to mine.

"Good to see you," I said with a nod.

"Good to be alive," Peter said with a toothless smile. He wasn't joking.

- - -

The days turned into weeks, and my routine never varied:

- Up at 6 A.M.
- Eat breakfast with the other rehabbers
- Help with breakfast for the homeless
- Help with deliveries or clean
- Eat dinner with rehabbers
- Go to chapel
- Help clean up after dinner for the homeless
- Go to bed
- Get up and do it again

A couple weeks later, Peter and I stood one night out on the mission's fire escape, looking up at the Denver skyline rising above the warehouse across the alley. Peter pulled heavily on a cigarette. I stood downwind, trying to stay out of the smoke.

"Rehab is a tough thing," he mused, looking at his cigarette.

"How do you mean?" I asked.

"I *think* it can work, but I don't know," he said. "I mean, look at me. I've been a coke addict for more than thirty years. That's not a drug addiction, it's a lifestyle."

Earlier, when I had met him, I told Peter that I believed he could come into the program, get clean, and "get on with his life." I realized in that moment how foolish a statement that was. Peter needed far more than to "get on." He had been a slave to drugs far too long. He needed a new path, a new hope, a new life, and a new Lord.

He took another long pull. "I mean, let's say I do actually graduate. It'd be a miracle, but let's say I pull it off. Who do I have on the outside? All of my friends are addicts. My landlord was my dealer, and I used to smoke crack with my boss. All my friends for the last thirty years have all been addicts. My whole life revolved around coke. Where am I supposed to go when I want to start over?"

Peter's question that night has continued to haunt me. *Where should he go?* Rehab is a good start, but a clean life for those men means much more than a simple decision to "just say no." A recovering addict has to get clean, then try to build a new life out of rubble.

In the movie *The Shawshank Redemption,* one of the prisoners, "Red," as he's called, says that men who have been in prison for a long period of time become "institutionalized"—unable to function in the normal world. They didn't know anything other than a life of crime or drugs before they entered prison. Then once inside, they become dependent on the structure that prison provides. Once they get out, they're set up to land right back in prison because they were never truly free.

What lay ahead for Peter?

I leaned back against the fire escape that night, wondering what the God of love had to do with all this. Christ offers us real freedom, eternal freedom in Him. Jesus says in Luke 4 that He came "to proclaim liberty for the prisoners." I sat there feeling a weighty, yet wonderful truth: some bonds in this life can only be broken by Christ.

"Peter," I said, slowly, still thinking through what I was going to say. "I believe it *is* possible for you to get clean and for you to graduate. But you're probably not going to be able to do that alone. You were trapped in your lifestyle—you just said that. I think that means that your only hope is outside of you, outside of your situation. Only Christ can set you free. Let His power work in you. Otherwise, your best attempts will leave you right where you started."

"Yeah," Peter said, taking yet another pull. "Everyone here keeps talking about that. Maybe for once I should listen."

The life of a recovering addict proceeds forward one moment, one decision at a time. The next morning Peter got a Bible from the intake chaplain and began reading.

THE BREAKFAST CLUB

About two weeks after I entered the mission, one of the main cooks (also a member of the rehab program) had to leave because he tested positive on one of the mandatory weekly drug tests. He had been in the program for nearly a year and had earned a pass to leave the mission every so often for an hour. During one of his outings, the temptation for heroin had become too strong.

The disappointing event led to a desperate need for another cook and somehow I got selected. The funny thing was that I had no idea how to cook, much less a meal for two hundred! My new job meant I would get up at two-thirty every morning to work alongside the other cook helping to prepare the first two meals of the day. We put breakfast on for the homeless at five, and then for rehab members at six-thirty. The lunch shifts came at eleven and twelve-thirty.

Getting up at two-thirty was quite a shock to my system (at college I usually didn't go to bed till later than that!). But working along with Trevor, the other morning cook, was memorable. About thirty, and a recovering cocaine addict himself, Trevor was short and built like a wrestler. He shaved his head to a shine every other day with mission-issued razors.

We made an odd-looking pair—one tall and lanky with

thick hair tied back in a ponytail; the other short, stocky and bald. Every morning, the first thing hundreds of men and women would see shuffling through our food line was the two of us in uniforms. We thought it was hilarious, but maybe it was one of those early-morning humor things.

At two-thirty sharp, Trevor and I would crank up a local Christian radio station and start down our list of preparations. During the slower songs we'd work without talking, each of us lost in his own thoughts and prayers. But when a faster song came on, we'd start yelling out the lyrics, playing air guitar on our industrial-sized spatulas, loving the fact that we were too far underground for anybody to hear.

Trevor had accepted Christ the day after he entered the mission. "My life was useless," he told me one morning as we cleaned up the kitchen. "I had no hope, and before I came here I'd been thinking a lot about suicide. I finally decided one day that things needed to change. The only One strong enough to do that is Christ."

- - -

The basement cafeteria was cavernous—about fifty by eighty feet, with high ceilings, and filled with large, round tables. I'd dish out scrambled eggs each morning to more than a hundred people who had been lined up since five to get breakfast—quite a change from the dining commons at school where I'd typically stroll in for an eat-all-you-want breakfast buffet at nine-thirty! This world was different. If you weren't here when we served, you didn't eat, period.

Every now and then, breakfast guests would get a little frustrated with our rules. Trevor and I usually served alone on the early shift with the homeless, before the other rehab members were even awake. Truth is, that ragged army could easily have stormed the kitchen and taken every last bit of food.

One morning, when we ran out of sugar packets, disaster struck. Some of the homeless would pile fifteen or twenty sugar packets into every cup of coffee. The sugar served as a temporary high for those who couldn't wait until their next fix. So when the brown cardboard box on the stainless steel counter turned up empty, one man erupted. Screaming, coughing, and turning bright red, he started yelling over the counter at us, using every foul word imaginable to convince us of our incompetence.

I wasn't sure what to do, but Trevor stared calmly over the counter at the man until he ran out of breath. Then he explained. "Sir, I'm sorry that we're out of sugar, but there will be more tomorrow. The shipment comes this afternoon."

"Whatever," the man said, and walked away grumbling.

But the unhappy customer wasn't finished. He began yelling at a couple seated at the table he wanted, telling them they had to leave because he didn't want them there.

"That's it!" Trevor said. "Mike, I need you with me." He threw off his apron and stormed out to the dining area to take charge. When the troublemaker saw us coming, he stopped yelling and started backing toward the wall, holding up his hands in surrender.

"Okay, I'll wait for the sugar," he whimpered.

"It's not about the sugar anymore, bro," Trevor said, fuming. "I was gonna let you stay here and enjoy breakfast, but now

31

you're starting crap with these guys. You need to leave."

"No I don't!" he said, turning hostile again.

"Yeah, you do, bud," I said, pointing toward the door. "You're more than welcome to come back at lunch. But if you mess with anybody, you're out. That's the rule here."

"You guys suck!" the man said, suddenly deflating, and heading for the stairs. Trevor and I followed to make sure he actually got out to the street.

"I hate doing that," Trevor said as we walked back down the steps to the cafeteria. "But if we don't, this place will turn into an absolute madhouse."

"You'd think he'd be happy just to eat," I said, shaking my head.

Most people were thankful. Enormously so. The rescue mission kept them alive—otherwise they'd be begging or scrounging for food in garbage cans.

This world was so completely different than the one I had known previously. Where I had known excess, I now saw only need. In my heart, I sensed attitudes of entitlement being replaced by thankfulness. My understanding of my world was being transformed, and so was I.

- - -

One morning, a guy came through the food line who could barely stand. The stench of alcohol on him overwhelmed me even though I was on the other side of the counter. Still, he somehow made it to a table where he sat down with several friends.

Trevor and I had turned our attentions to preparing lunch when suddenly the leftover cafeteria crowd started laughing. We walked out to see what was going on and were met with the sight of the drunk man lying limp on the floor, his face, chest, and legs splattered with his breakfast. He had passed out while eating, slid off of his chair, and pulled his tray of food down on top of himself.

We tried to wake him up, but all our shaking, slapping and yelling didn't evoke a response. So we called the paramedics. Then we carried him up the stairs to street level and laid him in the mission entry way to sleep until the medics arrived.

"Ah, another day," Trevor said sarcastically as we walked back to the kitchen.

- - -

A few days later, while Trevor and I were roasting several large chunks of lamb for a goulash soup, James, a rehab member, walked into the kitchen.

James had severe bipolar disorder and had moved in and out of prisons since he was a teenager. Most recently, police had arrested James in the process of manufacturing large amounts of methamphetamines in the basement of his home. A court sentenced him to a significant amount of prison time, which he could avoid if he entered the program at the mission and remained there until he graduated.

The mission medical clinic was trying to help James get his bipolar disorder under control. It was a process though, one that involved adjusting the medications week by week. Until his medications were stabilized, James's moods were unpredictable, swinging without notice between rage and sorrow, elation and depression.

"How's it going, James?" I asked as he walked into the kitchen and laid his Bible down on the counter.

"Oh, okay," he said flatly. I could tell he was having a rough day.

"What have you been up to this morning?" Trevor asked.

"You know," James said, shifting his weight from one foot to the other and looking at the floor, "I'm just really sad right now. It's like I don't know what's wrong. I'm just sad."

I was opening one of the one hundred cans of corn we would mix into that night's goulash. "Did you get your meds figured out?" I asked.

"Sort of. I'm better this week than last week. Still not completely though. They said I shouldn't be sad anymore. I'm sad now."

Trevor pointed to James's Bible. "One of my favorite verses is 'The joy of the Lord is my strength,'" he said.

"I like that one," James said with a nod.

"You should read some of the Psalms," I said as I opened another can of corn. "They talk about looking to God when you're sad or depressed or in a tight spot. They talk a lot about hope."

"I just read the Psalms," James said, picking up his Bible again and thumbing to the middle.

"Which one?" I asked, starting on another can.

"All of them," James said, looking up at me.

"All of them?" I asked, amazed.

"Yeah. I couldn't sleep last night. I was really sad. So I just started reading at Psalm 1 and ended this morning at Psalm 150. They're really good."

"Wow," I said, turning back to my work. I tried to remember a point in my life when I had been as honest about my emotions as James had just been with Trevor and me. I couldn't. For some reason, I hardly ever admitted when things weren't going well. Instead, I usually glossed over my struggles with an easy cliché like "it's all good" or "hanging in there" and thought nothing of it. Psalm 34:18 says "The LORD is close to the brokenhearted." I wondered if pretending you're not broken keeps God at a distance.

The men I was meeting were at the bottom—the worst point of their lives—and weren't afraid to admit it. But their ruin opened the way for honesty. Pretending didn't help anymore, and anyway, they didn't have the strength to keep it up. They just told it as it was, when it was. I found that part of living in ruin refreshing.

35

- - -

Sometimes after Trevor and I had finished the breakfast shift, we'd make ourselves eggs over easy and sit in the deserted cafeteria, drinking coffee, talking about anything and everything.

One day Trevor made an announcement. "We've got a group of kids coming in today to work with us."

"Yeah?" I said, wondering what he meant. Several volunteers had dropped in to help over the past week, but no kids and never a large group.

"Yeah," Trevor continued. "A youth group or something from somewhere, and they're going to be here all week."

"That's great," I said. "Do we have enough work for them?"

"Oh sure! They can clean up the storage rooms, peel pota-toes, serve lunch—on and on. We always need help if people want to work."

Sure enough, later that afternoon fifteen teenagers arrived from Nebraska. Over the next few days, I watched a subtle transformation happening in them, too. The kids moved from timidity and caution to comfort and confidence. By the end of the week, most of them were enjoying themselves, bring-ing a welcome gift of friendship and encouragement to the whole place.

Something critical is missing in places that care for the broken and needy if the only people there are also broken and needy. Without the presence of people in the rescue missions whose lives are not defined by addiction, alcoholism, crime, and mental illness, there is little positive influence. Chaplains and pastors can only spread themselves so far.

One day I watched a high school junior peeling potatoes for more than two hours with a fifty-year-old alcoholic named Ronald. Every now and then I'd see Ronald laughing or begin-ning to tear up as he listened to the student talk.

Later that same afternoon James told the teens the story of his journey through addiction, of the marriage he was los-ing, of the children he'd left behind when he went to jail. At several points, his eyes filled with tears. When he finished speaking, the students applauded James, then gathered around to encourage him. I wonder if he had ever experienced anything like it before.

If we are the body of Christ—and Christ came not for the healthy but the sick—we need to be fully present in the places where people are most broken. And it has to be more than just a financial presence. That helps, of course. But too often money is insulation—it conveniently keeps us from ever having to come face-to-face with a man or woman whose life is in tatters.

A bunch of high school kids from Nebraska showed me something important: When we're willing to get down to eating together, listening and telling the truth together, cleaning together, pealing potatoes together, the Gospel comes alive.

HELL FIRE

Every night about 150 ragged and torn men and women would pile into the chapel to listen to the mandatory service. The rule there, as at most gospel missions, was simple—you go to chapel before you get dinner. Everyone in the audience was dirty, hungry, desperate and broken. Pretty much everyone on the platform was not.

Out of all the 150 homeless, you might hear a couple getting involved in the service, offering up an occasional "amen" if the speaker asked. Many slept. Most just waited it out. After a full hour the air in the room was rank, especially if it had been raining as it often did on summer evenings.

Typically, a group from a local church with a heart for inner city outreach would come down to lead the service. Most groups would stand in front, obviously nervous, to sing four or five worship songs. Then a speaker would deliver a message.

The theme of their messages rarely varied—and it always began with bad news. For example, a speaker might begin with Romans 6:23—"The wages of sin is death"—and continue from there with vivid descriptions of the suffering,

37

pain, and remorse to be experienced in hell.

I couldn't help wondering why the speakers so often focused on the "hell, fire, and damnation" theme and so little on hope, joy, love, peace, or really *anything* positive. Did speakers assume that to be homeless or addicted means that you are definitely on the road to hell and only scare tactics matter now?

Think about it: If you see someone dangling precariously off a cliff you might warn them about falling to his death but it would make more sense to throw him a rope. Obviously the people standing in the front had good enough intentions, but our good intentions and sound theology are wasted if those we minister to don't feel that we care about their immediate concerns.

Jesus did thunder warnings of suffering and condemnation, but primarily to those who were convinced they were healthy and in no need of Him. To the weak, diseased, hungry, and sin-bound, He had another message. "Come to me, all you who are weary and burdened" (Matthew 11:28).

Of the twenty-seven chapel services I attended, about twenty focused on hell, condemnation, sin, and eternal suffering. Are each of these relevant parts of the gospel message? Yes. But are they the most appropriate parts to focus on with such a physically needy group?

By the end of my weeks at the mission, I decided the answer was probably not.

Late one evening, after yet another sermon about hell, an old man came up to me. He walked with a bad limp, had leaves stuck in his matted hair, and reeked of sweat and alcohol. He paused for a minute, swaying gently back and forth, then looked straight at me.

"I thought Jesus talked about love!" he blurted.

"He did," I answered with a sigh.

"Huh," he replied, perhaps a little reassured. Then his demeanor changed. "You know what really pisses me off?" he exclaimed, turning to shake his fist back at the stage. "That guy probably lives in a nice house and drives a nice car and has a nice life! Last night I slept next to a dumpster that smelled like urine! And *he's* gonna tell *me* about weeping and gnashing of teeth?"

With that he stormed off to stand in line for his dinner.

I remembered hearing someone once say, "You'll never scare anyone into heaven." I didn't completely agree at the time—the fear of God and the conviction of the Holy Spirit had helped bring me to repentance. But in the Denver Rescue Mission I began to see the truth of that statement. Telling someone who is suffering deeply that he's going to suffer more is probably a waste of breath. It's like warning someone who is already starving that they're about to get really hungry. But tell him of the restaurant that serves heaping meals to all who come no matter where they're from or what they look like, and he's more than likely to listen.

I thought of Christ's words, "For God did not send his Son into the world to condemn the world, but to save the world through him" (John 3:17). Weren't these well-intentioned speakers condemning the broken for being broken?

EXIT TO STREET LEVEL

Denver's skyscrapers towered above me, offices still lit at this late hour, and above them, stars in the night sky. The air was cool, a welcome change as I stood on top of the rescue mission surveying the world above and below.

Freedom.

During the previous month I had come to this same spot—on the mission roof—a few times just to keep from going stir-crazy. I had known the mission experience would be confining. After all, I was officially in a rehab program. Freedom to come and go as you pleased was only granted after you had proven that you wouldn't drink or do drugs outside the mission. Necessary, but still maddening.

Thus, one evening, while alone out on the fire escape where Peter and I had talked, I turned to look up at the stars and noticed an old steel ladder leading up to the roof. *Hmmm.* I looked back into the hallway making sure no one was approaching, then quickly hauled myself up the ladder to the roof.

The view was breathtaking, and it was the only place, except for the toilet stall with no door, where I could be alone to gather my thoughts. But this would be my last visit. I stood on top praying for Peter and Trevor and all the other men I had become friends with during the month.

My departure would be the buzz the next morning, as it always was when someone dropped out. I had debated it seriously, but ended up writing several letters to guys in the mission, hoping and praying that my leaving would not make others do the same.

Earlier I had wandered through the mission, and stopped at the security center to talk with the guards, who were also rehabbers. As I sat and talked, I watched the images from the various security cameras flickering on a TV screen in the corner of the room. It was 1 A.M. I had decided that at 4 A.M., I would walk unannounced out the front doors of the mission. The only good-bye would be my shrinking image fading on that small TV screen.

The mission had been an incredible experience for me. I had seen Christ piece lives back together, one day at a time. Change for an addict takes a lot of work, a lot of prayer, a lot of God—and usually more than one restart. Almost every day I'd seen setbacks. Watching men destroy a year's worth of rehabilitation with a single bad decision had been frustrating and painful. But even though the path to recovery was winding or interrupted, I *had* seen lives change.

I'd seen change in me, too. I had learned important lessons about living with people on the bottom rung of society—ways of phrasing questions, ways of cracking jokes, ways of showing respect and appreciation. At the same time I had gotten a little more used to the harshness of life all around me.

I stood there that night in my world of skyscrapers and stars, remembering the month—the early mornings, the crazy encounters, the frustrations, the conflicts. Of course, I had no idea when I walked into the mission my first day that I was going to become a cook, or talk to Peter at 2 A.M. about Christ, or encourage James in the middle of deep depression. But the Lord had directed my path. With every passing day I had found myself less anxious about what was to come, and more willing to trust in the One who knew.

I leaned to look one more time down to the waiting streets below. Then I backed onto the ladder, and clambered down into the mission. It was four o'clock, time to depart.

The sound of 150 homeless men snoring loudly made an

41

interesting chorus, not to mention a wretched stink. As quietly as I could, I dropped a letter at the locker of each man I'd written to. Then I went to my own locker, which still didn't lock, grabbed my bag, and walked out of the room.

Adrenaline pumping, I reached the main door without running into anyone. I paused, took a deep breath, pushed open the door, and stepped out into the night. Just before the door closed, I turned and saluted the security camera above the door.

It was colder on the street than it had been on the roof. I huddled down into my donated sweatshirt. But I was tired. Soon, even the most uncomfortable of locations seemed to beckon me to roll out my bag.

Dilapidated warehouses on either side began to give way to expensive shops. One was a glittering, four-story furniture superstore advertising a summer blow-out sale. A large curved glass window at street level displayed a massive king-sized mahogany bed piled high with soft white pillows.

Sale price: $1400.

I stood in front of the display like a kid in front of a toy store, separated from luxury by only a plate of glass, yet infinitely far away. I probably stood there for a full minute longing for the white comfort I saw in the window.

Then I was struck by the irony of it all. I rolled out my bag on the concrete right under the display window, curled up, and fell sound asleep.

In the morning, a store employee nervously prodded me awake. I started, and opened my eyes to bright sunlight.

"You've got to move on," the store guy said. "Sorry, man."

"Sure," I said, rising and stretching.

It was my first night on the concrete. My first sidewalk wake-up. And the first of many times I'd hear, "Sorry...you've got to move on."

The store guy kept an eye on me until I was out of sight.

WASHINGTON, D.C.

"Jesus promises a life in which we increasingly have to stretch our hands and be lead into places where we would rather not go."

HENRI NOUWEN, *IN THE NAME OF JESUS*

Start: July 1st, 2003
End: July 28th, 2003
Duration: 28 days
Locations: Downtown Washington, D.C., Georgetown

The night before we left for D.C., Sam debriefed me on his experiences at The Farm, the rehab facility (also run by the Denver Rescue Mission) where he'd spent the last month. Instead of being surrounded by concrete and sirens, Sam had found himself in the middle of pigs and corn. The men we had lived with, though, had been the same—the homeless, and a lot of recovering addicts who needed time away from the pressures of street life.

Sam called his time in rehab "a pounding and preparation." The pounding was what happened to his pride. "I wanted people to know I wasn't in trouble—I'd just come to learn about those who *were* in trouble." The preparation came, said Sam, as he learned to see that all of God's children (Sam Purvis included) are beggars at the foot of the Cross, broken people in need of mending.

In the middle of our conversation, my uncle called unexpectedly. He sounded quite matter-of-fact. "While you sleep in D.C., you're going to get stabbed with an HIV-infected needle," he said.

Thanks for the call, but not very comforting. Fortunately that never happened.

Most of the homeless people we encountered in the nation's capital were war veterans. Maybe they had arrived in town long ago to protest on one issue or another and just never left.

In D.C., almost everything is about power. It's the capital of power for both the United States and the world. Important and powerful people travel in bulletproof limousines to important places for important meetings with important people.

Of course, that didn't include us. We mostly hung around the Martin Luther King Jr. Memorial Library, just eight blocks east of the White House. It's an area where two worlds collide. Walking from one side of the street to the other was like walking across the burn line of a forest fire. In one block the scenery morphed from new high-rise office buildings and luxurious cars to old buildings and dirty streets. Two worlds side by side, each pretending the other didn't exist.

Washington formed the backdrop for our first experience of actually living on the streets. And it was no gentle introduction. Our first days and nights of homelessness were marked by long hours of panhandling, crowded feeding kitchens, staggering humidity, and cockroaches.

THE WORLD IS CHANGED

The traffic roared around as we stood near a busy intersection outside Union Station. Waves of heat radiated up from the streets and off the cars. It was a muggy, hot morning in Washington, just a few days before the Fourth of July. Sam and I had just arrived on the streets of our second city.

We had no idea where we were going to sleep, no idea where or what we were going to eat, and no idea where to go or what to do. We both felt overwhelmed, a little sick, a little afraid, and a lot alone. But we knew we were supposed to be there, and that made all the difference.

"How's your heart?" I asked Sam.

"Beating like mad."

"Mine, too."

For lack of anything better to do, we grabbed our packs and guitars and started off toward the food court in Union Station. It might make a good place to collect our thoughts. On the way there, we came upon an old man and woman sitting on the sidewalk, yelling and cursing at everyone who passed by. Every now and then, their performance evoked the horrified response they were looking for, sending them into fits of laughter.

"Here we are," I said to Sam under my breath as we walked passed.

There we were. Everything Sam and I had was stuffed in our packs and guitar cases. I wore a blue cut-off T-shirt and a tattered pair of pants I had cut into shorts. Sam wore a bright yellow T-shirt and shorts. Neither of us had shaved, we were sweating rivers, and the packs already seemed heavy.

Once we were inside and downstairs we grabbed a table in a corner. A small boy at the next table began crying, insisting

47

that he didn't want the piece of pizza his mom had just bought.

"You hungry?" I asked Sam.

"A little."

The hunger pangs start early when you're used to eating whatever you want, whenever you want, and then find yourself with empty pockets sitting next to a lot of food.

"To think that it's all right there—over those counters, in all those restaurants—and that we can't enjoy any of it," said Sam. "That's weird."

"Yep," I said, watching an employee heap a massive serving of lasagna onto a plate in the kiosk just across from us. "So close and yet so far away."

The mother in front of us, utterly frustrated with her young son, grabbed him by the hand, walked over to the trash can, and threw away the pizza untouched. Sam was watching, too.

"But I'm not that hungry," I said to Sam. "You?"

"Not yet anyway."

Sam got up to walk around a little. I began an entry in my journal. After ten minutes Sam returned.

"Hey, bud," he said, "there's a church giving out sack lunches today. I just talked to some people from a choir that's giving a concert there. We're invited."

"No way!"

"Yeah, they start in about an hour but it's a couple of miles from here, so we should get going. Now I'm hungry!"

- - -

This time when we walked out of the station, the homeless couple took notice of us and stopped their random assaults.

"Hey, you!" the man yelled.

"Yeah, both of you. Come over here!" added the woman.

I shrugged at Sam and we walked over to where they were sitting.

"Welcome to the streets of D.C.!" the man shouted at us, flashing a toothless grin. A mangy dog growled at us from between them until the man quieted it with a harsh command.

"You boys are new here," the woman said. "You just traveling through?"

"Sure are! I'm Mike."

"Mama," the woman said, holding up her hand.

"Greg," said the man. "Well," he said, standing and hitching up his pants, "as I said, welcome. If you're panhandling, go to Georgetown, it's a lot better over there. Breakfast at Zaccheus' Kitchen next to the library every morning except Sunday. Stay safe, and have a good time."

With that, Mama nodded, and yelled an insult at a businessman who was walking past deep in conversation with his cell phone. He shrugged, frowned, and looked confused, which sent Mama and Greg into gales of laughter.

We thanked them and walked away. "You believe that?" Sam asked.

"No," I answered. "Just because we look like we do, we're accepted as homeless!"

Looking at a small torn map, Sam and I made a calculation and started walking toward the church offering lunch. After about an hour we stopped in front of a small apartment to ask a frail old lady for directions.

"Oh!" she said, clearly shocked that such scraggly men were asking for directions to church. "That church is about four miles that way," she said, pointing back down the street we had just walked.

49

Great! I thought. My pack felt like it was full of rocks and our water bottles were completely empty. This was going to be a long day. No, this was going to be a long four months!

We thanked the woman and started off again. An hour later we arrived back at Union Station and went inside to fill up on water.

"Didn't expect to see you again so soon!" Mama yelled as we passed, her dog still barking.

"Neither did we!" Sam called with a smile.

"We got a bit lost, but we're back on track now!"

"New boys in a big city," Greg said to himself, loud enough for us to hear.

It was mid afternoon before we finally made it to the church, a large old gray building. As we walked inside, hot and exhausted, we heard a choir singing. We found the choir rehearsing in a small gymnasium. After waiting for the song to end we walked in and found a corner where we could listen.

When their concert was over, choir members gathered around us to talk. They were high school kids from Texas, and excited to be giving us lunch. "Here you go!" two of them said excitedly, carrying up a box of sack lunches.

"Thanks," Sam and I said together, happy to pull out a lunch.

"Take two," a guy said. "We made too many!"

"Land of plenty," said Sam, reaching into the box again. I grabbed another sack, too, and shoved it into the top of my pack.

While Sam and I were finishing our bologna sandwiches washed down with warm Pepsi, the group packed up their things and waved good-bye. As the last person left, Sam and I sat there wondering what to do next.

"That was quick," Sam said.

"Yeah," I said. "I think we're going to have a lot of quick relationships while we're out here. We're going to say hello and good-bye within an hour quite a bit. But I doubt if there's going to be a touring high school choir giving out sack lunches at every church."

After we shouldered our packs and walked out, we heard the janitor locking the church doors behind us. A church is just a building if there's no one in it.

- - -

It was getting to be rush hour, and the number of people on the streets had increased substantially. Sam and I stopped at a busy intersection, both of us feeling shamed by the reason we had stopped. It was time to beg.

I slung off my pack, setting it down flat on the concrete in order to use the sleeping bag as a seat. Propping open my guitar case, I grabbed the guitar and sat down. I was sweating and I felt my face turning red with embarrassment. This was a moment we had both dreaded.

Begging is hard. It's something you expect hungry dogs to do, but not men and women made in God's image. The minute you put out your hand, or open your guitar case, it feels like you're writing "failure" and "weakness" all over yourself. You're telling everyone who comes by, "I am unable." The message blares up and down the sidewalk, and across multiple lanes of traffic. And the message doesn't stop screaming until you pull back your hand, or close up your case.

On our first go at it, panhandling was almost too humiliating to bear. We began with "In the Secret," normally a fast paced, excited worship song. But we didn't feel excited. And anyway the noisy street seemed to swallow our music whole. Gradually, song by song, we added volume and confidence.

In his book *The Ragamuffin Gospel*, Brennan Manning writes, "We are all equally privileged but unentitled beggars at the door of God's mercy." I thought of that as person after person walked past without donating or even making eye contact. I felt my frustration rising until I realized how unentitled I really was. No one *deserves* mercy. And no one walking by owed us a dime. Mercy is, by definition, undeserved, or else it isn't mercy.

Every coin in the case looked different after that.

- - -

52

After nightfall, Sam and I ended up back outside Union Station near a large fountain. The area was surrounded by smaller courtyards that looked like as good a place as any to spend the night. Three or four other street people were snoring loudly around the fountain, so we chose one of the nearby courtyards and stretched out our bags on the red bricks.

The scene had quieted from earlier. But as we settled down, the scenery changed yet again. Cockroaches started appearing, greedily exploring the landscape with their long antennas waving in every direction. Then, I caught sight of a long black rodent scurrying along the railing behind our packs. I jumped up yelling, determined to kick the rat. Sam did the same, but our commotion sent the rat running.

"This is lame," Sam said, looking at the cockroaches scurrying around.

"I bet they smell our food," I said, rummaging around in my pack for the second sack lunch. My sandwich had gotten nicely smashed by my poor packing job. We sat there in silence, slowly chewing slightly stale bread and warm bologna, keeping an eye out for the roaches, and throwing pebbles at them whenever they emerged.

"I can't decide if I want to sleep on top of my bag to escape the heat or inside my bag to escape the roaches," said Sam as he finished his sandwich.

I laughed. "Ah, choices."

"Hey, here's a prayer I've never prayed before! 'Lord, please keep the rats, cockroaches, and any other fun little things off us while we sleep tonight.'"

"Ha!" I said, rolling over. "It's like Greg said earlier today, 'Welcome to the streets.'"

53

Concrete is hard. Everybody knows that, but trying to fall asleep in the courtyard that night, I was actually living it. I rolled over every ten minutes or so, trying to alleviate the parts of my body that were going numb.

I thought about Mama and Greg and wondered how many nights they had spent on the streets, cockroaches and rats scurrying around them as they slept. How could they do it?

The rest of the month in D.C., the four other cities, the remainder of the trip—it all stretched away in front of us like an eternity. It felt like Sam and I were boys who had swum far out to sea and only on deciding to swim back had noticed how impossibly far away the beach really was.

"Jesus, be our Rock. Truly," I prayed silently and closed my eyes.

"YOU LIKE CHICKEN PARMESAN?"

Sam and I sat next to each other in the hot, humid air, leaning against the wall of a two-story restaurant. The sun had set an hour ago, but the buildings and sidewalks still radiated heat. The bricks behind our backs burned like an oven. The street in front of us was filled with thick fumes and the roar of traffic. My head throbbed with what was probably a dehydration headache.

I reached into my pack and pulled out the water bottle, grateful for the last drops of warm water. Every now and then the door to the restaurant behind us would swing open and let out a gust of air-conditioned coolness seasoned with the inviting aromas of Italian cooking and the sounds of friendly conversation.

Sam and I started talking in a dazed sort of way about cool restaurants, tasty Italian food, and tall iced drinks. But every time a bus rumbled by, we stopped. When you're tired, hungry, hot and thirsty, every word takes effort.

Occasionally a passerby glanced down at us. Mostly though, they just stared straight ahead, trying hard to pretend we weren't there. A cluster of teenage girls walked past. Then they turned and came back to the door of the restaurant to read the menu.

While they laughed and traded opinions among themselves, one of the girls leaned in toward the menu. Silently she mouthed "Chicken Parmesan," and "Linguine Alfredo." But then she frowned, spun around, and pushed her way past her friends. "Nothing looks good," she declared in a high whine.

"Yeah, it *all* looks bad!" chimed in two of her friends as they hurried to join her, and the cluster moved away down the sidewalk.

I turned to look at Sam, my mouth hanging open. Then we both laughed, shrugged our shoulders, and went back to staring silently out into the hot street.

Fifteen minutes later, I asked. "Are you hungry?"

"Yeah," said Sam. "More thirsty though. You?"

"Same." I agreed. "We should go play the guitar somewhere soon."

"Yeah."

But finding the energy to move seemed impossible. "I want to eat" no longer meant just walking to the refrigerator or ordering off a menu. Every sandwich demanded hours of sitting on the hot cement, playing and singing, trying to be heard above the noise of the street. And on this afternoon, exhaustion from walking everywhere, the dehydration of living outside, and the lack of sleep from being constantly moved by the police and security guards had taken a toll. So we just sat, half-aware, watching people ignore us.

It seemed like the perfect pastime.

Suddenly a young family came into view. The dad—dressed in T-shirt, shorts, and a baseball cap—walked in front, but he was looking down, evidently listening to his wife. She came along behind pushing the stroller. As they rolled up to us, a small boy in the stroller looked out at me.

When you're sitting on a sidewalk, you're at eye level with babies and kids. It's a different world down there. As toddlers stumble past holding their parent's hand, they lock you in their unashamed gazes or they peek curiously out from their strollers. They haven't yet learned to ignore what they see, so they can actually take in the world as it is. While kids might pretend people who don't exist do, it's the parents who pretend that unwanted people who do exist don't.

I held the boy's gaze for a while and gave him a smile, which he immediately returned. From high above him, his mother said something that caught my attention. "We have to be about the gift of giving and the wisdom of the Holy Spirit," she said.

I looked up quickly, wondering what those words might mean, what with us sprawled on the sidewalk not five feet from her. But when I caught her eye, she looked away and quickened her pace.

Now the family was well past us. But the boy in the stroller still looked straight at me. The further away they got, the further he leaned out, looking back, fixing me with his grin and a steady gaze.

That seemed like the gift of giving to me.

We sat for another couple of minutes, trying to gather the strength to get up and earn our meal for the evening. Suddenly the restaurant door burst open, bringing the familiar smells and sounds. But then a large man wearing a tuxedo stood in front of us. "You've got to leave now, guys," he announced. "You're killing our business. With you out here, no one wants to come in."

"No problem," I said. I knew it would happen sometime, it always did.

"No problem," Sam echoed in a monotone. "You got it."

Without another word the man marched back inside, mission accomplished, taking the aroma of dinner and the laughter of friends with him.

We struggled to our feet and reached for our packs. "That's okay," I said, groaning under the unwelcome weight. "We need to go play anyway."

"Yeah," said Sam. "And besides, my back was starting to cook."

We picked up our guitars and set off down the sidewalk.

"Do you like Chicken Parmesan?" I asked.

"No. Not really."

"Me either."

MOST IMPORTANT MEAL OF THE DAY

Breakfast is the most important meal of the day, especially when you didn't eat the night before.

In D.C., the only place we found to get breakfast on Sundays was at an Episcopal church in the heart of the city. The old church's oak pews were at least softer than concrete and seemed almost welcoming after a night on the sidewalk.

Each morning, a female priest spoke briefly on the passage of the day while more than a hundred homeless men and women sat scattered through the sanctuary, enduring the mandatory service. Some rocked slowly back and forth. Others talked to themselves or coughed incessantly. Some slept quietly, others snored loudly. Some escaped to the sounds of heavy metal in their headphones. Some actually listened, and you'd hear an occasional "amen" ringing out through the expansive sanctuary, usually well after the priest had begun her next sentence.

One Sunday, the priest offered communion, and about forty of us ragged souls walked up and kneeled down around the pulpit.

I knelt next to a huge man who had been seated in front of me. His broad shoulders and large, rough hands told of a lifetime of hard labor. The wrinkles in his weathered face were thrown into dark relief by the dirt that had collected in them. His long graying hair and beard were stained and thick with debris.

As I knelt beside him, he started coughing violently, a thick gurgle rising from his lungs between convulsions. He braced himself against the floor with both hands until he could regain his composure, then he wiped his eyes, shifted back to a kneeling position, and waited.

The priest moved quietly around the circle, leaning down to each person. "This is the body of Christ, which was broken for you," she said, looking each in the eye. Then she came around again with the cup. "This is the blood of Christ, which was shed for you." The white of her cloak shone brilliantly against our filth.

By the time she brought the cup to the big guy next to me, he was back on his hands again, struggling for breath. She stopped directly in front of him and waited for him to rise. When he could look up at her, she held the shining silver cup as he put it to his lips. I heard him swallow, and as he handed the cup back to the priest, two drops of wine ran down his mustache and disappeared into his beard.

The priest wiped the cup where he had received and stepped in front of me. "This is the blood of Christ…"

I'd never taken communion on an empty stomach before. The cup burns when you're hungry. It goes deeper, quicker, when there's nothing to stop it.

The priest moved on, and with a deep sigh, the big man next to me crossed his chest and pushed himself to his feet. I rose, too, and before we walked back to our seats, we caught each other's gaze and nodded.

- - -

My call number that morning was 124, which meant I'd be the 124th person to be served breakfast that day. A long wait, but we were hungry. Sam was number 125.

He dropped into the pew behind me and we both began journaling amidst the homeless buzz of the sanctuary.

Ten minutes passed.

Twenty-five.

An hour later, number 123 was called. My big communion partner rose to walk forward. Then Sam and I got called and we walked forward, too, to give our names and social security numbers to the church worker at the door.

At the next number, 126, we heard a yelp and laughter from the back of the church. Looking back, we saw a tall man, deeply bent with age, limping hastily down the center aisle. He only wore one shoe, which seemed to be on his good foot.

It was Josh, a guy we'd met just before the service. When Josh reached the man collecting names and numbers, he paused.

"Name and social security number?" the monitor asked.

Josh replied, or seemed to, but what he actually delivered was an incomprehensible torrent of words in no particular order. The monitor simply shrugged and drew a line through the box next to Josh's number.

Then Josh spotted Sam and me. "Hey!" he called out excitedly.

"Hey, Josh!" Sam and I both said, turning to greet him. Josh was clearly delighted that we remembered him. Sam asked how he was doing.

"Well…," Josh said thinking for a moment, then he launched into a five-minute volley of more garble. Whatever he was saying took so much effort that a lot of spit came flying out at the same time. Along with the awful stench of his breath.

We kept what distance we could, while doing our best to

listen. When Josh finally stopped, I gave him a huge smile and said with as much enthusiasm as possible, "That's amazing!"

By now the line had snaked closer to the kitchen and we could smell breakfast. But then we heard disheartening news. "Gentlemen," a deep voice announced, "we're out of orange juice and biscuits this morning."

Of course, eating for free at a mission or a church means you aren't really in a position to complain. But, man, it was a bummer to walk into the dining room and see others with two glasses of orange juice and three biscuits! The leftovers for us were green scrambled eggs, grits, and lukewarm water. Still, I was so hungry that even the grits looked superb.

Or at least they did until the four of us—Josh, the big guy, Sam and I—sat down at the same table, and Josh let loose with another muddled diatribe aimed at the big guy. With Josh to my right, and the big guy across the small table one seat to the left, the direction of Josh's torrent of words and spittle was directly over my breakfast.

I laid down my fork in disgust. First, no biscuits or orange juice. Now, the fine mist of Josh's spit piled up on my arms, my tray, and my grits.

Sam looked on amused while I tried to shield my food from further damage. When Josh finally ran out of gas, I wiped off both arms with a sigh, looked at Josh, and said, "Is that so?" I was no longer in a mood for manufactured enthusiasm.

Nothing left to do, I figured, but grab my fork and dig in. And I did.

As Sam and I were leaving, one of the kitchen crew was scrubbing tables with a steaming rag that smelled strongly of bleach. I noticed another server about to empty a plate with two biscuits on it into the trash.

"Hold it!" I yelled, pointing to the biscuits. "I'll take those!"

"You sure?" she said as I walked over. "They're half-eaten."

"Yep. Couldn't be happier," I said with a smile, grabbing both of them and shoving one into my mouth. On the way out the door, I gave her a muffled thanks over my shoulder.

A hungry man can be a fast learner. When you come to a table with nothing but need, you are grateful for things you might have pushed aside before. And when you kneel, hungry and broken at His table, you receive a grace from Him you might, at some other time, have completely missed.

You'll know this grace when you take it. It goes deeper, quicker, and it burns all the way down.

A SONG FOR PAMELA

Sam and I were leaning up against a building trying to come up with a plan when we noticed Pamela.

She spent a lot of time near the Martin Luther King Jr. Library, too. Her particular mental disability seemed to leave her tortured with fears.

On this morning, Pamela was walking toward us as if to start a conversation. Then she turned away, uncertain, then turned back to try again. As she approached, she wrung her hands, and her expression changed constantly from anxiety to eagerness and back again.

Finally she got close enough to speak. "H-h-hey guys?" she stammered, almost turning to flee at the sound of her own voice.

"Hi, Pamela. How are you today?" I said, trying to be as reassuring as possible.

Pamela relaxed enough to ask her question. "Can you play me to sleep again tonight?"

"Huh?" Sam and I said, exchanging confused glances.

"Can you play me to sleep tonight? It really helped last night," Pamela replied. "I fell right asleep when you guys played." She was trying both to smile and plead at the same time.

"You could hear us last night, Pamela?" asked Sam. "We didn't see you around."

"Yeah, I was over by the library. You were playing the guitar and singing and I fell asleep. It was nice. Can you do it again tonight?"

I asked her where she was sleeping now. On the other side of the street from us, she said, near the construction. "I sleep on a bench. Timothy, my friend, watches out for me. He's nice. Do you know him? Will you play for me tonight?"

Pamela's demeanor had changed to anxious and fearful again, and her childlike request was impossible to turn down.

"Sure, Pamela," I said. "We'll play for you again tonight. Just listen carefully while you're falling asleep and I'll bet you'll hear us."

That evening we played as darkness fell over the hot streets. The lyrics to "Hungry," one of my favorite worship songs, seemed fitting:

> *Hungry I come to you,*
> *for I know you satisfy.*

It was a relief to play and sing for the joy of worship rather than for our dinner. I wondered that night if maybe God hadn't brought us across the continent just to sing Pamela to sleep on His behalf. The apostle Paul said in Ephesians that God works that way—that we've been created to keep certain appointments for Him, to complete certain tasks (maybe even with a guitar as darkness falls).

After we'd finished "For Your Arms Are Open Wide," Pamela stood up and shouted a long "Thank you!" across the street. She waved and smiled until she was sure we'd seen her. Then she lay down on her metal bench to sleep.

WE HAVE A POLICY

Sam took off on a walk for some alone time—a luxury we tried to allow each other at least once a day. It helped keep us sane. I ducked into a coffee shop, bought a cup, and sat toward the rear of the building hoping to blend in so I could read and journal.

Unfortunately, I didn't blend in very well. I just couldn't hide my stained and tattered clothes or my rank odor. After about an hour, an employee approached to ask what I was doing.

I pointed to my journal and book. "I'm just working on some things—journaling and reading."

"This area is for customers only," he said flatly.

"That's okay, man," I said, picking up my coffee cup and sloshing around the remains. "I bought this cup of coffee."

The employee shook his head. "Customers only," he said more harshly than before.

"But I *am* a customer," I protested, still holding my cup.

The man glared. "No, you're not," he said.

"What do you mean?" I asked, frustrated. "How do you define *customer*? You sell coffee here. I bought coffee from you. Now I sit here drinking it. How am I not a customer?"

"How long ago did you buy the coffee?" The guy was obviously running out of patience.

"About an hour ago," I said, glancing at a large clock on the wall.

"Ah," he said, shaking his head. "We have a forty-five-minute drinking policy."

"What?" I couldn't believe what I was hearing.

"You heard me. You have forty-five minutes to finish your coffee and leave. You're fifteen minutes overdue." He was getting angrier with each sentence.

"Look," I said pointing to our packs. "I'm here with a friend, and he's out taking a walk right now. He should be here any minute. As soon as he returns, we'll be gone. You have my word."

"How long till he gets back?" the man asked doubtfully.

"Ten, fifteen minutes," I said, praying that Sam would get back sooner. Disgusted but appeased for the moment, the employee left.

About ten minutes later Sam walked in. "Great walk," he said.

"Bad news," I said, hopping up and heading to my pack. "We need to leave. Grab your stuff."

"What do you mean?" Sam asked, taking a seat. Just then the employee came back. "I thought you said when he got back, you would leave."

"Just packing up," Sam said, getting up.

"But why do we need to leave?" Sam asked politely.

"We have a no backpacks allowed policy."

"Wait a minute," I said. "I thought you said that we'd been here too long and violated the forty-five-minute drinking policy!"

Sam jumped in. "And a no backpacks policy in a *coffee shop*?"

"Yep. That policy is brand-new," the man said coldly. He turned to stare at me. "So is the other policy. Now *leave!*"

He spun around and swaggered off. Sam and I pulled our stuff together.

"Wow…" muttered Sam, cinching down his bag.

"Yeah," I said. "Got to love the policies around here."

Once outside, we decided to set up our mobile guitar shop down the street near a stoplight. We sat on the sidewalk, pulled out our guitars, and tried to tune over the traffic noise.

For the next half hour, to an accompaniment of horns, trucks, and loud pedestrians, we played some of our favorite songs. When we had pulled in enough money for dinner, we decided to close our set with "Shout to the North," an upbeat worship song we could play better than most in our repertoire.

As we finished the first verse, a woman in her late twenties who had walked past us twice stopped to talk.

"Are you guys Christians?" she asked.

Actually, Sam and I hadn't been asked that on the street yet. "Yeah," we said simultaneously.

"Then what are you doing on the streets?" she asked, looking confused.

"There can be Christians on the streets," Sam said. "Are you a Christian?"

"Definitely," she replied. "For a few years now. You guys hungry?"

A few minutes later, the woman was treating us to a full meal at a Chinese restaurant a few blocks away. Her name was Tiffany, and she was a local college student who was on her way from her job to a class. She made time in her busy schedule to bless us, though, and what a blessing it was. The lunch was incredible—crab wontons, sesame chicken, egg-drop soup. It was the best food we'd eaten in a long time. Of course we didn't know it at the time, but during all our months on the streets, Tiffany was the only person to take us out to dinner.

Back out on the sidewalk, the three of us gathered for good-byes. "Tiffany, I don't think 'thank you' is enough," I said. "You don't know how much you've blessed us."

"Yeah," Sam agreed. "'Thank you' just doesn't cover it."

"Well, you're welcome. But I should be thanking you. I'm encouraged more than you know—and I just had dinner with two homeless guys!"

While pedestrians streamed by, the three of us stood in a circle and prayed together, thanking Him for the community of believers, a Body that extends far beyond church walls and comfortable neighborhoods.

After the "amen," Tiffany stepped back. "Okay, who are you guys, *really*? I've worked in shelters before and I've never met guys like you!"

Sam and I looked at each other for a moment. We had known that such a question would come and had thought a lot about how to respond.

"Give us your e-mail address and we'll send you a letter explaining everything," said Sam. "But we can't tell you right now. It's…well, we have a policy."

COWBELL DOOR CHIME

One weekday afternoon, Sam and I walked into a D.C. sand-wich shop to escape the blazing heat of the streets. It was a perfect getaway—an empty restaurant with only the hum of the air conditioner. The cowbell over the door interrupted the silence and announced our presence.

A stairway led to a second floor dining area, where we found a corner table. Shrugging off our packs and laying down the guitars, we sat down across from one another, relieved to be out of the heat even if only for a moment.

After cooling down for a bit, I walked back down the stairs to fill our water bottles. I could feel the employees behind the counter staring at me. "How's it going today, guys?" I asked cheerfully. All I got in return were stony stares. My enthusiasm hadn't quite worked.

Back upstairs, as I threw Sam's water bottle to him, I became aware of a horrible stench rising from either Sam or me or our bags or all of the above.

"Bro, you smell horrible!" I said, making a face.

"Are you kidding?" Sam said with a laugh. "When you sat down I could hardly breathe!"

"Yeah, how long has it been since we've showered? Like, three weeks? That's terrible!" We both laughed this time. I think the air-conditioning was making us giddy.

"You know how you usually can't smell yourself, even if you wear cologne or something?" Sam said. He tried to take a fast whiff of his underarm, but he couldn't get within three inches before jerking away.

"Yeah."

"Well, you *know* you reek when you can't bear your own stench!"

"In high school basketball I always forgot to wash my practice jersey over the weekend," I said, still laughing. "By the end of the season it was stiff as a board. We used to smack each other on the back with them before practice."

"My team did too!" said Sam. We were really howling now.

"Look at this!" I said, standing up and pointing to the armpit of my shirt. It had now dried in the air conditioning and turned into ten inches of rock-hard fabric.

Even Sam was disgusted. "That's terrible!" he yelled.

67

Just then several people walked up the stairs carrying lunch trays, but when they caught sight of us, the lead guy hesitated. Sam and I looked down feeling ashamed that we had caused him to pause, our smiles disappearing. I sat down and pulled my bag closer, trying to give the group as much social (and breathing) space as possible.

The man regained his composure and walked over to the furthest table from us. A girl took a seat with him, while another couple sat one table away.

When another guy walked upstairs, he, too, went to the far side of the room and plunked down his tray. On it I noticed a meatball sub and a worn brown leather New Testament. Soon all five, obviously strangers to each other, were busy eating their sandwiches.

I pretended to be reading a book, and Sam did the same, but the aroma of that meatball sub was killing us.

After a couple of minutes, one of them asked the man with the Bible what translation it was.

"NIV," he answered. "What version do you read?"

"NLT," the guy answered.

"Really?" the girl from the other table chimed in. "I really like the NASB."

"I guess it's just a matter of preference," the guy in the middle said, taking another bite of his juicy meatball sub. The next ten minutes were filled with lively conversation between the five new friends. Across the room, Sam and I sat quietly, reading and reeking.

Eventually the five ate their fill and crumpled up their wrappers. Getting ready to leave, the man with the Bible told both couples he would pray for them. Both couples thanked him honestly and said the same thing in reply. As they walked past us, Sam and I looked up, trying to catch their eyes and nod a hello. But they carefully looked away. Each emptied their tray of garbage into the trash can next to Sam and turned to walk down the stairs.

I remembered many times I had walked past a homeless man or woman sitting on the cold sidewalk, awkwardly averting my eyes and whistling to cover my discomfort. I wondered if those men and women had been as frustrated with me as I now was with the people who were walking down the stairs.

As they walked out the door, the cowbell rang loudly, and reflections of sunlight flashed through the downstairs portion of the restaurant. After that, we were alone again—empty restaurant and the hum of the air conditioner.

"Did you see that?" I asked Sam, nodding to the trash can.

"Yeah," he said with a sigh. "There's probably a whole sandwich between those five wrappers."

"Yep. You hungry?"

"Sure am."

Sam looked over his shoulder at the trash can, his sudden movement causing a couple of flies to start buzzing around the lid. Sam looked back at me and shrugged.

"Here we go!" I said, rising up and lifting the lid. As I did so, several flies buzzed lazily away.

We both grabbed what looked like more recent trash and, pushing our books aside, spread it on our table. My big find was the remains of a club sandwich, only slightly mushed. I took a huge bite and started chewing, trying not to think about where the sandwich had come from or who might have had the first go at it.

Sam had scored the remains of the man's meatball sub. I asked him how his lunch tasted.

69

"Good!" he said through a full mouth. "Yours?"

"Good! That first bite was a little shaky, but it's easier now. I'm hungry, so that always helps."

Just as we were finishing the last scraps of our meal, the sandwich guy from downstairs walked up the stairs and stopped. "You guys need to leave," he said, staring at us blankly.

"Okay," Sam and I both replied, getting up and crumpling the sandwich wrappers for the second time. By this time we were used to hearing people say those words. They were always delivered in the same monotone.

I decided to shoot for the moon. "Hey, man," I said, trying to sound congenial, "do you guys ever throw away food? You know, when you close, do you throw stuff out?" While I asked, I made a show of pushing my twice-crumpled wrapper deep inside the trash can, appearing as interested as possible with the treasures buried within.

"Um…" The guy became fidgety and looked away. "No, we don't throw anything out. We keep all of it. The bread, the meat, the cheese, the vegetables—we keep them all fresh and then we use them the next day. Sorry."

"No problem," I said. "Just curious."

Sam and I were headed for the front door, where the cowbell would let the sandwich crew know they could finally relax. But just then the fire alarm went off. An ear-piercing siren filled the restaurant with din while white strobe lights flashed over our heads.

We looked around expecting to see flames. Turns out the sandwich guy supervising our departure had leaned against the wall and accidentally pulled down on the red alarm switch. We could see him swearing in the clamor.

When we walked out, the cowbell barely registered above the noise. Two fire trucks were already rolling up.

A restaurant emptied? A whole city block filled with the wail of sirens and clamor of alarms? We shook our heads and kept walking. It's amazing what two smelly homeless guys can accomplish in one afternoon.

LIKE A CHILD

It took a while to figure out the best times and locations to panhandle. A good choice meant cash for food. A bad one could mean no cash and no food. In the early stages of our journey, as you'd expect, we made mistakes.

We discovered, for example, that good acoustics didn't count for much. If the location and time were right, we could bring in a decent return over the roar of trucks and buses. (Maybe our music sounded better if you could hear it less.)

71

The one consistent factor was foot traffic—the more people passing by, the better. And the promise of a lot of people passing by was what brought us to a sidewalk on the Potomac River waterfront in Georgetown one busy Friday evening.

Georgetown—the neighborhood in D.C. where the rich and powerful came to enjoy the rewards of their success.

We staked out a place on the boardwalk. Behind us, yachts were lined up at their moorings in the river, with large parties taking place on several. In front of us, hundreds of people milled around, waiting to get into posh bars and restaurants.

We figured we'd struck gold, and started to play.

Hours later, Sam and I were in a deep funk. The humidity had turned us into sticky globs. Thunder growled in the distance. And we only had eighteen cents for our night's work. Our prime panhandling spot had turned into another bust. But why? Happy crowds milled back and forth on the boardwalk, many dressed in expensive clothing and jewelry. Patrons listened from outdoor tables. Strollers stopped occasionally to listen. But no one seemed to notice the open guitar case at our feet.

Finally, I set down my guitar and looked over at Sam. "What's going on, bro?" I asked, exasperated.

No sooner had the words escaped my mouth than a group of ten or so school kids came walking along the waterfront. One of them saw our guitars and called the group over. But as soon as they had surrounded us, it became clear that they, too, had hit the streets with a mission. They were a baseball team for a Boys and Girls Club of America, and were trying to raise money for new uniforms.

"Can you help us out?" their leader asked.

I looked from our earnings to the young entrepreneur and sighed. "Well, we've got eighteen cents, bro. It's yours if you want it."

Just then I noticed a commotion at the back of the group. A small boy was trying to elbow his way forward. When he finally got past his friends and stood in front of me, I could see that he looked concerned.

"You don't have any money at all, do you?" he said.

"Ah, no, bud. I don't," I said.

He began digging around in his pocket. His friends seemed to hold their collective breath, while around us, the lavish restaurant, bar, and yachting scene rolled on. Then the boy pulled out a dollar bill and a quarter and dropped both into my case.

"Don't worry," he said, "I got you covered." He turned and pushed his way back through the group. Silently, one boy after another on the team turned away, too, and began filtering away down the boardwalk.

I'll admit, it took me a while before I could speak. I found myself laughing in amazement. I was even too amazed to be hungry anymore. "I think we're done for the night," I said, even though we still didn't have enough money to eat.

Sam agreed, and without another word we packed up and, leaving the glitter behind, headed to a nearby park to find a place for the night.

Later that night, the storm that had been threatening all evening unleashed its torrents on the city. Thunder drummed and lightning flashed. Sam and I had to move under a nearby freeway overpass to try to stay dry. But even that didn't work too well, and we ended up soaked.

73

The thing is, every now and then in that soaking, hungry dark, one of us would start laughing again in amazement at that young kid's gift. We were still amazed in the morning as we spread out our bags to dry. I'm still amazed today.

I saw that boy several other times along the waterfront— I guess he and his friends had also found that it was the best time and place to panhandle. Nearly every time he came by, he'd try to drop something in our case—sometimes a dollar, sometimes a dime. If we turned down his offer, he would look confused. If we accepted, he looked satisfied and confident—like he'd just wrapped up the best business deal of the night.

Paul suggests in 2 Corinthians 8 that God gives us wealth so that, by giving it away, others will be amazed by God's goodness and give Him thanks. Our wealth might be a dime.

But if we do it right, the one we give to can be amazed for years.

A street kid in Georgetown taught me that.

SEED MONEY

A thick red sun settled slowly into the horizon, and the world shifted to softer tones. It would take a while for it to cool, though. I wiped my forearm across my brow, and it glistened with sweat. I looked over at Sam who was also sweating heavily in the muggy heat. Playing and singing so people will notice you takes a lot of effort.

We both took a drink from our water bottles.

"Think we'll get another thunderstorm tonight?"

"Yup," said Sam.

We picked up our guitars again.

"'Trading My Sorrows'?" I asked.

"Hit it."

Soon our music was again blending in to the waterfront ambiance of conversations, car horns, boats, sea birds, traffic. Crowds of people ebbed and flowed, and some stopped to listen, but no one added to the meager sprinkling of coins in the bottom of my guitar case.

We called it seed money. Spread out a few dimes, nickels, and quarters to invite more giving. But you have to be strategic. Put in too much and passersby will think you're doing just fine without their help. Don't put in enough and they'll assume you're losers—no one else wants to help out, so why should they?

Well, that was our working theory. For whatever reason, people generally need a nudge—to get in the right mindset—before they'll help out someone at the bottom. But on this night, either the music or the theory wasn't working. Our seeds refused to multiply.

The location had seemed perfect, too. About twenty yards away, a line of happy people waited on the boardwalk for a ferry ride. For ten dollars, they'd get an hour-long cruise up and down the Potomac, accompanied by a guide's commentary on all the historically significant buildings.

During the chorus, I noticed that a woman sitting on a bench with her family was singing along. Her eyes were shut, her hands lifted. Her response was encouraging. On such a hot night, the worship of even one other person was refreshing.

When we finished the song, she walked over to say thank-you. "My husband died four years ago. I haven't heard that song since his funeral," she said. "Thank you." With that she turned, wiping away tears, and walked back to her children.

"That's the good stuff," I said as she walked away. It seemed our seeds were producing a harvest of another kind.

- - -

The ferry arrived, and the lineup of families eagerly got on board. Sam and I watched, wondering aloud why we still hadn't made any money.

"'Thy will be done,' isn't it?" Sam said.

"You mean like right now? When we pray before we start panhandling, pray for provision and still make nothing?"

Sam laughed. "Yeah. Now is a perfect example."

That got me thinking. "I think I often pray 'Thy will be done' not really meaning that," I said. "I think I mean more often, in all honesty, 'Thy will be done because I already know what I'm doing today.'"

"What do you mean?" Sam put down his guitar.

"When I wake up in the mornings I say 'Thy will be done' in prayer, and though I mean it to a point, my daytimer is already full. Barring something strange, I know where breakfast, lunch, and dinner are coming from. I know who I'm meeting with, where we're going, and what we'll talk about. There's not much uncertainty in *any* part of my day. But out here…" I said, pausing to look around, "out here, 'Thy will be done' might mean we don't eat, or we get jumped, or we get sick, or whatever."

"Yeah, sort of different, huh," Sam said. "It's like trust means something different when you don't feel in control."

"Yeah, different. But you know what? I can't believe how good it is."

"How so?"

"We're alive, we're okay, we're being sustained, we're meeting people and having incredible experiences—albeit some good and some miserable. But we're living what *His* will means, that though we may go hungry or not achieve something we want, He has His way, grows us as He sees fit, and shows us what He wants us to see. Imagine if we were to forgo all of this just so we could have clean clothes or a refrigerator full of food."

"That would depend. Full of what kind of food?" said Sam. We both laughed.

- - -

Dark clouds had piled up over us by now, but we talked on. We agreed that our own ideas and expectations tended to make us deaf to hearing God's will. We needed, at least at times, to just lay them down and listen. Leave the next move entirely up to God.

By the time the ferry returned, and everyone began to walk off, we heard the first rumble of thunder. The solo worshiper and her family walked past us, and we exchanged waves. Soon we had the boardwalk to ourselves again.

When lightning flashed nearby, Sam and I decided to pack up. Looking down at our few lonely coins, he whined, "I don't think they like us."

"No, they *hate* us!" I said, as dramatically as possible. Suddenly, I had an idea for dinner. "Hey! There's a movie theater over there about a half mile. It's getting nearer to closing time. I bet we could score some popcorn."

"Old popcorn for dinner?" Sam didn't sound impressed.

"It's better than nothing," I said. We decided to give it a try and started walking.

When we got to the theater, I stayed outside with the gear while Sam went in to scout popcorn. We had noticed that we were more welcome if we did our begging alone, without a backpack and guitar. I sat on the theater steps. I could feel the power of the approaching storm charging the night air with electricity.

A few minutes later, Sam emerged carrying two small boxes of popcorn and dragging a black garbage bag overflowing with the stuff. At the same moment, a hard rain swept down on us.

"Great!" Sam yelled, sarcastically. "Soggy popcorn is even better!"

We struggled to take our gear and our dinner to the shelter of a nearby overpass. The rain came in torrents, lightning flashed, and thunder shook the city. Above us on the freeway, traffic slowed and horns honked in the downpour. But Sam and I stood there feasting, happy to have a front row seat for the show—and popcorn, too.

"This is amazing," I said, taking another mouthful.

"Yeah," Sam agreed. "Way better than a movie. You can feel the thunder right in the center of your chest."

I thought back to when I was a boy, stretched out on my front lawn in Colorado to watch thunderstorms envelop my small town. The incredible forces of nature at work, the danger and excitement of the advancing storm. I'd watch entranced until Mom found me and called me back inside to keep me from getting electrocuted.

I finished my box of popcorn and smacked my lips. "Ugh," I said.

"What?" Sam asked.

"Ugh! You know that weird feeling when you walk out of a movie and your lips have gone numb because of all the salt on the popcorn? I've got that going on right now. I need some water."

I grabbed our bottles and walked back to the theater. Careful not to meet the questioning glares of the security guard, I hurried straight to the men's room to fill up. Then, on the way back through the lobby, I cruised by the condiment counter and grabbed a few packets of relish. When I got back to the overpass, I handed two to Sam.

"Your side of vegetables," I said.

"Are you kidding?" Sam asked, looking down at the plastic packets in his hand. "You call this a balanced meal?"

"Hey, I'm still hungry. Anything helps."

We both shrugged and forced down two packets apiece. But even with plenty of water, we gagged. When you're still hungry, the aftertaste of pure relish is pure torment.

"Where do you think we should sleep tonight?" Sam asked, taking another long drink of water.

"Right here," I said, trying to calm my stomach with another handful of popcorn.

"Under the overpass?" Sam asked

"It's dry," I said with a shrug.

- - -

About an hour later, my stomach churning uncomfortably with the unusual dinner I had eaten, I lay awake thinking about the day. It seemed such a random thing that a passing woman would be so blessed by our music. Many things had to happen in a specific order for that one experience to transpire, from my crazy idea to live homeless to Sam joining me, to our being on the waterfront at that exact moment while she waited for the ferry. Too many "random coincidences," if you ask me. Praying "Thy will be done" means you don't believe in chance.

My thoughts drifted to a conversation we'd had in a soup kitchen a couple of days earlier. We had just sat down to a meal of spaghetti when a man named Jake came up to stake a seat across from us. He did so by slamming his tray so hard on the table some of his spaghetti sauce slurped up through the air and landed with a splat.

"You guys new here?" Jake had asked, looking intently back and forth between us. In between bites we introduced ourselves. Jake seemed to think we were in the wrong place.

"What do you mean?" I asked, cautiously.

79

"Look around," Jake said. "There are two hundred people in here. One hundred and ninety-seven of them are black. Then there's that old white man over there with no teeth and you two. So who are you? What are you guys up to?"

"We're traveling," I said, wondering if our cover had been blown. "You know, panhandling and moving from city to city."

Jake squinted for a moment and with his expression changing from skepticism to satisfaction, picked up his fork and began to eat. "So, how are you guys surviving?" he asked. "How are you making money?"

"We play guitar," said Sam.

"Are you in a band?"

"Not exactly. We just play on the streets at night."

"You do alright?" Obviously, Jake had something on his mind he was pushing toward.

"We do alright, I suppose," said Sam. "Better in Georgetown than here."

Jake looked around with a wry smile, then leaned toward us, motioning for us to lean in, too. "Here's what you do," he said. "Let me tell you how to make two hundred dollars a day. You'll love it. Go somewhere and get a pair of old, ratty clothes that you don't want. You guys already look bad, but you could look even worse. Tear holes in them, rub them in the mud, make yourself look absolutely terrible. Then, go sit outside Union Station at rush hour. Hunch your back, cough a lot, make your eyes water."

Jake paused to laugh, then he continued. "When people stop—and believe me they will—make up a sob story. Your mother got killed when you were two. Your father raped you. You've got AIDS. Your girlfriend just died three days ago. Go on and on, making them believe stuff even *you* can't."

Apparently I didn't look impressed. Jake raised his eyebrows in disbelief. "Guys!" he said, leaning in even further and dropping his voice to a conspiratorial whisper. *"People give me twenties and fifties all the time!* Imagine how much crack that'll buy!"

Then, to complete the drama, Jake stood up, grabbed his tray, and walked away limping theatrically.

I don't doubt for a minute that Jake consistently did what he explained to us. Some people maliciously leech off the needs of the have-nots for their own purposes. They manipulate the guilt of the haves believably enough and get whatever they want.

In Denver, I'd heard of a guy on the streets nicknamed Father Fraud. He was rumored to drive a Lexus and live outside the city in a nice home. Every night he came downtown in an old coat and old boots to beg with a Campbell's soup can. He made ninety thousand tax free dollars a year.

Were Sam and I any different than Father Fraud or Jake? That question was troubling.

I stayed awake thinking about it long after the storm had passed us, almost until the concrete outside the overpass was dry. Homelessness was a choice, not a necessity for us. But, our panhandling, our seed money, we didn't use that money for drugs or nice cars. We used it to survive. "Thy will be done" was answered for us, at least in part, by how much our seed money grew. I decided that leaving God room to provide by singing for our supper was not manipulation. As long as Sam and I weren't maliciously ripping anybody off, living under the cover of homelessness wasn't wrong. A little crazy maybe, but not wrong.

Just before the sun began to lighten the sky to the east, I

drifted off to sleep, hoping Sam and I would never have to eat popcorn and relish for dinner again.

PHOTO OP

One night in D.C. Sam snored softly as I lay awake reading by the light streaming from the windows of the Martin Luther King Jr. Memorial Library. This place had become a favorite refuge. Hanging out in the city's public buildings helped us escape the heat and humidity during the day. And using the bathrooms whenever we wanted, to get a drink or brush our teeth, seemed like a genuine luxury. At night we often slept near the library's main doors, under a big overhang that helped make us feel a little more secure.

As I lay there reading John Perkins's book *Let Justice Roll Down,* I noticed a group of twenty-somethings walking past. They stopped, looked in our direction, and then turned to talk among themselves. Amused, I put down my book and watched, wondering what could possibly come next. It wasn't often that people stopped to look us over, especially at night.

Soon one of the group seemed to get nominated, and the others pushed him out in our direction. He walked over sheepishly, hands in pockets.

"Hey there!" I called out.

"Hey," the guy said, looking embarrassed.

"What's up?" I asked. The guy's friends were watching us and laughing.

After a self-conscious pause, he got his request out. "Uh, can I take a picture of you guys?" he asked.

"Huh?" I said. "Why?" I was confused.

"You're an interesting part of the city," he said quickly. He sounded like he was trying to let the word *interesting* imply that Sam asleep and Mike awake were in the same league as, say, the Jefferson Memorial.

"Part of the city?" I responded, sounding as dumb as I felt. I couldn't believe what I had heard. So now we were just scenery. Well, at least interesting scenery—like the statues and monuments of the capitol, like the animals at the zoo.

But scenery?

"Sure," I said, still flustered. "Sure, why not?"

"Thanks!" the guy said, relieved. Then he lifted his camera, leaned forward, and flashed Sam and me in digital color. When he got back to his friends, they surrounded him, eager to see what this particular piece of the American dream looked like up close.

I'll tell you what it looked like. One grungy sleeping bag zipped around a large sleeping figure. And one grungy man, sitting up, awake and flustered, clutching *Let Justice Roll Down*.

As they walked away, I shoved my book into my pack and rolled over. "You've got to be kidding!" I said out loud, disgusted. But no one was listening, not even the scenery.

83

PORTLAND

> *"The exclusion of the weak and insignificant,*
> *the seemingly useless people from everyday Christian life*
> *in community may actually mean the exclusion of Christ;*
> *for in the poor sister or brother, Christ is knocking at the door."*
>
> DEITRICH BONHOEFFER, *LIFE TOGETHER*

Start: August 1st, 2003
End: August 27th, 2003
Duration: 27 days
Location: Downtown Portland, Waterfront Park

'd rather be cold than hot. But in Portland, as Sam and I huddled under bridges trying to stay warm and dry, I frequently reconsidered that preference.

Homeless life in Portland struck us as quite different from Washington, D.C. In D.C. most of the homeless were over fifty, African American war veterans, and typically kept to themselves. In Portland, most of the homeless were in their teens and twenties, and they tended to travel in groups.

The general feel of the city was different, too—more relaxed, not so caught up with status and power. We had more open conversations with homeless men and women and more interactions with people as they walked past. Of course, the city wasn't swarming with tourists either, which meant we were viewed less as scenery and more as people. That helped our panhandling significantly.

Portland was easier to transition into but harder to endure. Sam and I struggled more to get along, for one thing. And our assumptions of what it meant to be a Christian got rocked by an unusual encounter.

By this time, Sam and I were getting more acclimated to life on the streets, and smarter. With every lesson learned and every step forward, we sensed that God was preparing us for what lay ahead.

THE IDEA OF COMFORT

Our first afternoon in Portland—clear, warm, and gorgeous—was a far cry from the typical stories of Portland's constant rain. Along the Willamette River, people walked, jogged, or rode bikes. A dog barked ferociously at a sprinkler, occasionally trying to take bites out of the stream of water.

Sam and I rested under a large tree in a waterfront park and felt at peace. As one hour became two, our journaling and reading made us sleepy, and we both stretched out on the grass to snooze. To make things even better, I had found a large root sticking up out of the ground to use for my pillow.

Just as I was dozing off, a cyclist in a helmet and racing clothes rode toward us. The black Lab running alongside him decided to come over to say hello and drool on me. When the bicyclist noticed, he cursed and called his dog away—not to guard our privacy, it turned out, but to express his disdain for the human trash the dog was investigating. When he saw the tree root under my head, he said, "Oh, that looks *real* comfortable."

I sat up. I had just been insulted by a stranger because of my choice of a pillow? I couldn't help but laugh.

The funniest part, though, was that I thought the tree root—hard and gnarly as it was—*was* comfortable. I was happy to find it! The shade was inviting, the grass was cool, the root was cozy.

Well, almost. Comfort is relative, a truth that was slowly sinking in. Days and nights in the open turn you jaded and numb. You get hungry enough and food from the trash looks appetizing. You get exhausted enough and the sidewalk can almost feel like a down-filled mattress. And compared to sun-baked concrete stinking of gasoline, garbage, and urine, a tree root in a park can feel like heaven. You forget how crazy your life must look to some urbanite whizzing by on his Italian racing bike.

Two nights later, I would have given anything for the comfort of that tree root.

Sam and I were sleeping under a bridge over the Willamette. A steady rain had been falling for hours. I awoke at some point in the night to the sound of the massive steel structure above us groaning and popping in the wind. And that's when I noticed a lake of rain water advancing toward us.

Great! I thought. *Sure will be fun when that gets here!*

Maybe I was just too tired to believe that it actually would, because I rolled over, pulled my bag over my head and fell asleep. Where could we go, anyway? The whole world was flooded.

Sometime early in the morning, I had the odd sensation of something falling off my head and running down my scalp.

I jerked my head up to see that the lake had arrived, carrying with it a disgusting mass of water-born cigarette butts, cans, leaves, pigeon feathers, and other trash. I was soaked through, and a heavy sludge now caked my face and arms and the outside of my bag. The stench made me gag.

Forcing myself not to throw up, I struggled out of the soggy bag, thankful for once that Sam and I hadn't eaten the night before. It's easier not to throw up when your stomach is empty.

What to do?

I walked out into the rain, shaking cigarette butts and leaves out of my hair and wiping the sludge off my face. Then I spread out my arms and looked up. Cold, clean water from the sky. Drop by steady drop it began to wash away the filth.

It was a moment I'll remember.

I wasn't angry having to shower in the rain. I wasn't frustrated by my circumstances. After a minute or two, I hardly minded the filth. Was I arriving at Paul's state of contentment "whether with everything or with nothing" I had talked about with so much idealism in clean clothes over coffee back home? Or was exhaustion simply taking its toll?

Maybe the reason so many people, Christians included, are so discontent is that we hold too elevated an idea of comfort, too grandiose a notion of pleasure. That sets us up to get frustrated by every passing circumstance. We can end up focusing more on our circumstances than on the One who ordains them.

When you get to the bottom—when getting rained on is a welcome solution to getting buried in muck—there is immense contentment in letting go of comfort.

"Don't worry about tomorrow." Just be thankful for now.

Cozy up to that tree root.

Let it rain.

WORSHIP UNDER A BRIDGE

About a week later, a drop of water fell from high above and smacked me on the forehead. When I opened my eyes and looked up, the evening stars had given way to heavy clouds. Portland's skyline painted their undersides in a pale amber.

Another drop of water hit the wood next to me with a louder slap. Then another. And another.

Sam and I were stretched out on a dock at the far edge of a marina in the Willamette River. Suddenly I heard the rush of rain advancing toward us across the river, and as it drew nearer, drowning out the sound of traffic on the freeway high overhead.

"Sam!" I yelled, scrambling out of my sleeping bag and hurrying to collect my stuff. "Sam!" I yelled again, "We gotta go! Now!"

Sam slowly stirred, but as soon as he heard the rain approaching, he hit high gear. In seconds, we had our packs on and were running towards the cover of the Hawthorne Bridge a couple hundred yards away. Despite our best efforts, the rain overtook us.

By the time we trudged under the bridge, we found it crowded with homeless men and women huddled in cardboard boxes. They sneezed and coughed. When we didn't see anyone we recognized, Sam and I decided to keep going down river. We finally found a dry spot under a flight of stairs.

We crawled under the stairs and spread out our bags. As long as the wind didn't blow too hard we figured we could stay dry.

Just as I was drifting off, Sam jolted up and announced, "We need to go back under that bridge, bro!"

"What's up?"

"I just had a rat two inches from my face! I woke up and it was looking at me!"

"Really" I asked, amused. "A rat right there in front of you?"

"Yeah! It was flippin' huge! I say we go back to the bridge." Sam was not in a mood to negotiate, and I was too exhausted to argue. Once again, we gathered our belongings and headed for the bridge. Fortunately, by then the rain was slacking.

As we reached the bridge, campers were leaving in droves, some jumping around to try to warm up. We plunked down our stuff near three guys who were staying, and one of them asked, "What kind of guitars do you guys play?"

"Yamaha," I said. "Simple but good."

90

I opened the tattered case, which was held together with duct tape and staples. The guitar itself was scratched and covered with grime. The strings had taken on an odd, thick sound, I think from the dirt that had worked its way into the windings. I handed over the instrument, and the guy began to play.

"What's your name, man?" I asked.

"Brian," he said, stopping for a moment to shake my hand. "Good to meet you."

"Likewise," I said. In the background, one of his friends was trying to wrap himself more tightly in cardboard. The other was packing a colorful glass pipe with marijuana. After about five minutes, the guitarist handed my instrument back to me.

"What music do you play, bro?" he asked.

"Actually we only play worship music," I said.

"Huh?" said Brian. "You mean like Jesus stuff?"

"Yep," replied Sam.

The guy with the dope let out a laugh and lit up, inhaling deeply and staring at me through the smoke. I thought I'd try to make friends anyway.

"I'm Mike, man" I said, extending my hand in his direction.

"Slant," he said, doing the same. "Good to meet you."

"Well, let's hear something," Brian said, encouragingly.

Sam and I laughed. "We're honestly not very good. We usually just mess around."

"That's okay. I'm no good either," Brian said.

Sam grabbed his guitar. As we tuned up, Slant inhaled deeply again, and held his breath for a long time. We started to play the Jars of Clay's song "Worlds Apart."

We sounded terrible, and I broke a string in the middle of it, but Brian didn't notice. He closed his eyes and tapped his foot to the music. We finished with a final strum, letting the music fade away into the sounds of rain and the river.

"That was amazing," Brian said, his eyes still closed. He took the bong from Slant and inhaled deeply. When he offered the pipe to Sam, Sam declined. "No thanks. We don't smoke."

Brian's eyes opened. "You guys don't smoke? And you only play Jesus music?"

"Yep," we said, nodding.

"Huh…," mused Brian. He thought a while, pulling back the pipe to get a better look at it. Then he handed it back to Slant.

"Hey, can you teach me to play that Jesus song?" he asked.

SUGAR MAN'S GOSPEL

Portland was the best city for panhandling. On some weekend nights we pulled in more than we needed for the entire week. Sam and I found we could survive on three dollars per day by eating at the rescue missions and riding the free trains around downtown. On busy evenings we pulled in as much as forty dollars, and put excess funds toward Greyhound tickets to our next city.

But after we had saved enough for bus fare, we struggled for ideas of what to do with the rest. We ended up deciding to use it to buy food that would help us build friendships among the other street people. Friends are good to have, especially on the streets.

One sunny day we walked into the dusty park under the west end of the Burnside Bridge carrying five extra burritos from a nearby Mexican restaurant. We started talking to Bruno and Theresa, a young homeless couple we had met a few days before outside a pizza shop that threw out leftovers every night just before closing.

We pulled out burritos for ourselves and gave them both burritos as well. They were amazed that we had bought extra with the intention of sharing. Their excited yells drew over another guy, who gladly accepted and quickly devoured a burrito, and left. About five minutes later, he came back and tossed a small zip lock bag at our feet. The bag contained two tightly packed nuggets of marijuana.

"I take care of those who take care of me," he said.

"Bro, thank you," said Sam, "but we don't smoke." He handed the bag back.

The guy was dumbfounded. "Ah, well, that's cool," he said finally. "Thanks for the burrito."

Just then, a ragged cheer went up as a bearded guy wearing a floppy canvas hat and a bright tie-dyed shirt skated into the park. He was singing loudly and balancing a large cooler on the front of an old, beat-up dolly. Poking out of his ragged shorts were unnaturally skinny legs attached to clown-sized shoes.

He stopped in a shady area near the center of the park, opened his ice chest with a wave, and proclaimed, "Open for business!"

"That's Sugar Man," said Bruno, disinterestedly. "He knows everybody."

People wandered over to rummage around in the ice and pull out cold sodas, placing crumpled dollar bills into Sugar Man's hand. He was selling twenty-five-cent soft drinks for a dollar. Not a bad business.

He stood there by his dolly and ice chest in the center of everything, yelling hellos and pushing his goods for about ten minutes. When business slowed, he convinced a woman lying under a nearby tree to come and watch his ice chest so he could visit.

Sugar Man began wandering around the park talking to different groups, spreading cheer wherever he went. It was amazing to see so much life come from such a small, thin man. Everyone seemed to know him and appreciate him.

After about fifteen minutes, Sugar Man made it around to us. Bruno and Theresa introduced him and he sat down, eager to get to know someone new. We offered a burrito, but he declined. "Too many Coca-Colas," he said with a wink over his shoulder to the woman standing by his cooler. His laugh revealed badly decaying teeth.

"Of course," he continued, "I've done more drugs than you can name. But since we're talking about names and times, and lives and rhymes, who are you and where'd you from come?"

I found Sugar Man absolutely fascinating. His sentences were as colorful as his shirt, the words twisted together, lyri-

93

cal and a little crazy. Listening to him felt like being stuck in an odd dream during an afternoon nap—I felt like he *should* make sense, but I just couldn't imagine how. He jumped from topic to topic, connecting freedom and Hollywood, the nearby river with the president. Suddenly he landed back on the subject of the burrito.

"Hmmm," he sat thinking. When he pulled on his scarce beard, the skin on his face sagged.

"What's up?" I asked as the uncharacteristic silence stretched on.

"Why did you offer me a burrito? I don't know you, you don't know me. Why, I wonder?"

"Thought you might be hungry," I said.

"Naw! That isn't it," he said. "Well maybe part of it, but you weren't selling me a burrito. You were *giving* me a burrito. These people are thirsty." With both hands, he made a sweeping motion around the dusty expanse. "That's why I sell sodas here. Because they're thirsty. But you knew I was hungry and you offered to give me food. Why?"

"Well…" I hesitated.

"You're Christians aren't you!" Sugar Man suddenly exclaimed. Eyes wide, he pulled the floppy edges of his hat down around his ears and leaned forward. "Aren't you?"

Sam and I nodded.

Sugar Man let out a whoop, stood up, spun around once, and sat back down. "So tell me about your journey," he said, taking off his hat, seemingly settling in for a long story.

Sam and I looked at each other a little bewildered. No one from the streets had ever asked us that. But over the next few minutes Sam and I explained where we had come from, how we had become Christians, and then described in general terms that we felt called to travel on the streets for a while.

"That's good, that's really good. These streets are rough. They take their toll on you..." He trailed off, his mind drifting.

"What's your story, Sugar Man?" Sam asked. But Sugar Man just stared blankly into space.

Suddenly he leaped up and began pacing back and forth, really worked up about something, breathing hard. "You know what my story is?" he yelled. "It is the story of David and Goliath!"

Sugar Man then proceeded to act out the biblical account for us. Every movement was filled with so much energy and drama that others wandered over to witness the one-man show. After ten intense minutes in which Sugar Man picked up and threw stones, enacted cutting off Goliath's head with a stick, and wept face down over his failure as king, he stood to address his audience. Looking every listening man and woman in the eye, Sugar Man said, "And the moral of the story, kids, is that David had to learn to trust God. So do all of you."

With that he pointed to those watching, took a bow to the loud applause, and came back to sit down again with our group.

"You guys are my brothers in Christ," he said. "I know it. The Bible tells me to love my neighbor as myself. Not even my brother, but simply my neighbor. You share more with a brother than simply with a neighbor and I'm supposed to love a neighbor more than myself. So, brothers, those I love more than neighbors, more than myself in fact, what do you need? Anything I have is yours because you call Christ Lord same as I do. You need a car? I've got one. It's yours. You need cash? I'll give you everything I've got. Place to stay? We'll work that out. So tell me, how can I serve you?"

While Sugar Man talked, Bruno had been packing a large glass pipe with marijuana. When he was satisfied, he and Theresa lit up. Bruno took a long pull and handed it to the person seated next to Sugar Man. Just as Sugar Man finished asking how he could serve us, he got the pipe, smoked it, and offered it to us. We both shook our heads, causing everyone to pause.

Sugar Man let out an exasperated sigh and filled the air with thick smoke. "You guys don't smoke?"

"Nope," I said.

"You guys do *any* drugs?"

"Nope."

"Amazing," he said, shaking his head and chuckling. "Amazing." Then he reached for the pipe, took another enormous pull, and sat back. His eyes glazed over.

Sitting there with Sugar Man, I felt my carefully established definitions of a Christian crack and expand. Here was an admitted addict and user openly proclaiming Christ in his community and asking how he could serve us.

What do you do when a good tree bears bad fruit or a bad tree bears good fruit? Look harder.

What's your definition of a Christian? Is it broad enough to encompass the drug dealers, pimps, prostitutes, and broken people of the world? Jesus said that he came to heal the sick. Drug addicts are messed up just the same as liars are messed up, just the same as all humans are messed up. We all need Jesus. We all struggle with personal ways in which sin plays itself out in our lives.

What's worse? To do dope or to not love your brother? Why do we kick drug users out of the church while quietly overlooking those who are ignoring their own different but equally destructive sins? Why do we reject the loving, self-sacrificing, giving, encouraging, Jesus-pursuing drug addict but recruit the clean, self-interested, gossiping, loveless churchgoer?

Which one do you suppose Jesus would rather share a burrito with under a bridge?

BODY BASICS

Most of us don't think much about bathrooms, or soap and water, or finding a meal or a safe place to sleep until we're faced with doing without. Then almost nothing else matters.

What Sam and I quickly learned living on the streets is that these daily basics play a huge part in defining both a person's social status and self-respect. No bed, no shower, no toilet equals no dignity.

Think about it next time you walk past someone huddled in a doorway. It's the easiest thing in the world to decide that the woman or man huddled there is *choosing* to dress in rags and reek of urine and body odor. Their choice, of course, means you can't be blamed for ignoring her or him. The person doesn't want to be pleasant, so you don't need to care. At the very least, you don't have to respond as you would if it were your mother or your brother huddled there.

Right?

But the fact is any one of us would look about the same if we were in the same place—having survived on the same sidewalks in the same cast-off clothing for months. Even more so if we wrestled alone in that doorway day after day with a substance addiction or a debilitating mental impairment, or both.

Sam and I found that almost every day on the streets became a dawn-to-dark quest for the simplest human necessities:

97

Where can I eat?

When you're hungry you stop worrying about what your food looks like, or what might actually be in it, or even how it tastes. You're simply trying to fill your aching gut.

The feeding kitchens around town were usually the best option. Depending on where they were located, and where we happened to be, breakfast might mean a forty-five-minute walk, lunch a one-hour bus ride, and dinner a two-hour wait in a line. The food was actually pretty good most times—a main course alongside salad, bread, fruit, and some sort of drink.

Unfortunately, prime panhandling time collided with feeding time at most rescue missions. That often left us eating fast food. Trust me, a steady diet of cheap burgers turns into another kind of starvation very soon.

Occasionally, pedestrians gave us their restaurant leftovers. Twice, people offered to buy us a meal. We also learned to dive into the trash without flinching, especially right after we saw someone discard something edible.

All in all, we learned to pray "Give us this day our daily bread" from a whole new perspective.

Where can I sleep?

Our first night on the streets in Washington, D.C., Sam and I had a long discussion about whether the best way to deter an attack would be to sleep in a well-lit area where we could see danger coming, or in a dark corner where fewer predators could find us. We usually picked the well-lit, high traffic option in hopes that if we got jumped, at least somebody might call the cops.

As it turned out, though, we were usually too exhausted

to care much where we slept—except according to the rules of the street:

1. Don't sleep in someone else's spot.
2. Find a place where you can sleep as long as possible.
3. Try to stay out of the rain.
4. Try to stay away from the rats.

Good sleeping areas routinely got cleaned out early in the morning (before the acceptable crowd showed up). For example, every night that we (and up to a dozen others) slept outside the Martin Luther King Jr. Memorial Library in D.C. we got a 5 A.M. wake-up call. A library security guard with a megaphone would shout, "Morning, gentlemen! Time to move on!"

Waking up refreshed didn't happen much, if ever. Some nights we moved three or four times. Rats, roaches, rain, stench, flooding, hecklers—there were so many reasons. We learned to sleep with one ear always listening. Traffic and car horns didn't wake us, but the sound of a rodent scurrying over our packs or rocks crunching under a person's boots forty feet away did.

One of the best places to sleep in Portland was near the southern end of Waterfront Park, which runs along the Willamette River. Here, near the Hawthorne Bridge, a cement patio offers a bedroom with a view up and down the river. But the metal railings mattered more to us than the aesthetics. We'd sleep with our packs wedged behind us and our guitars lashed to the railing with nylon webbing so that if an intruder tried to steal something, we'd wake up. Us on one side of our stuff, and—twenty feet straight down—the river on the other. That felt safe!

We learned such strategies the hard way. While sleeping on the steps of an old Catholic church in D.C., I had awakened in the early hours to find a guy rummaging in my backpack not ten inches from my head. Apparently he didn't like the first items he found—some books and my Bible—so he kept rummaging, and that's what woke me up. As I jolted awake, he grabbed a sweatshirt and took off, tripping over my pack and scattering my belongings. From then on, Sam and I took more care to sleep defensively.

How do I stay clean?

Actually, it's amazing how much our definition of *clean* changed. We transitioned from the typical (semi) frequent showering habits of respectable college students to, well, something far less. Having no soap or hot water probably helped things along. The longest period I went without a shower was nearly five weeks.

Most rescue missions have the resources to provide drop-in-visitors with a toothbrush, toothpaste, and other such items. But finding a place to use these things can be a challenge. Restrooms at fast food joints provided our best chances for a quick scrub.

Sam and I hardly ever did laundry during the trip. If we did it was because a rescue mission offered laundry services or because it rained and we couldn't get out of the downpour. One afternoon in San Diego, when our stench had become unbearable, Sam and I ran into the surf clothes and all. At least the stink of sand and sea water was more tolerable.

In every city except San Francisco, Sam and I stayed in a homeless shelter at least one evening. The shelters require every guest to shower before going to bed, which was a welcome blessing, although it meant crowding into small industrial-strength showers along with a dozen other homeless men.

Where can I go to the bathroom?

This most elemental requirement of the human animal often defeated us. What do you do, when you can't—like I couldn't—several evenings in D.C.—find a restroom? Well, you look for bushes or trees, even though they can be sparse in the heart of a city. You look for a corner behind a dumpster.

Other options included fast food joints, coffee shops, movie theaters, or public buildings. The major disappointment here is that employees who want to protect their facilities from people like you have complete say over whether you get access. They might let you in. They might tell you to get lost. They might tell you to "just hold it" even though you have diarrhea. So before you go in, you pray hard that the toilet police are having a good day and feeling generous toward the wretched of the earth.

101

What happens if I get sick?

We didn't like to think about it, and Sam and I took no medications along. You'd think that the constant exhaustion, exposure to the elements, and unsanitary conditions would have made us ill often, but the opposite was true. Sam and I only got significantly ill once. Those days were a low point though. All I wanted to do was sleep but security guards, car horns, and the need to panhandle or get to a feeding kitchen prevented that.

- - -

Every now and then, several of the body basics converged ("collided" is probably a better description). Then, look out!

One night in Portland a rainstorm sent us searching for cover. We ended up under the Hawthorne Bridge again, hoping to find a dry spot to sleep out the rest of the night. But the only dry spot under the bridge was the same place we'd used for a toilet the day before. A lot of other street people had used it for the same purpose, too, because the stench of the place was simply staggering.

What to do? Sam and I looked at each other, shrugged, and tried to roll out our bags as far as possible from yesterday's yellow puddle without sinking into tonight's mud puddle. Best just not to think too much in these circumstances. Best to put something over your face, breathe through your mouth, and try to sleep.

102

About a week later, in the same general vicinity, I awoke at three in the morning with my bowels in full rebellion. No matter how hard I tried, I couldn't get comfortable, or get the gurglings to subside. In fact, they got worse. I lay there, wide awake, dreading what was befalling me. At home, or even a rescue mission, you simply pull yourself from the comfort of your bed and stumble hurriedly to the bathroom. But not under a city bridge at three in the morning.

When a particularly urgent cramp hit, I sat up only to be hit by another horrifying thought. I had no toilet paper. Desperate, I rummaged through my backpack for anything that could serve as a substitute. Nothing. Then, as the discomfort crossed new thresholds, I let out a groan, grabbed my only other pair of boxers, and ran toward a large planter in the middle of the square. But at the last minute, I decided it was much too out in the open. So I shifted course and ducked behind some shrubbery.

It was a very long night.

I won't go into details, but let's just say don't ever wander through the bushes near the Hawthorne Bridge.

- - -

An ongoing struggle to find safety, a place to sleep, a bathroom, and food becomes dehumanizing for anyone. One experience at a time, a person's sense of dignity and sense of self-worth gets stripped away. I don't know what the experience would be like for someone who has lived on the streets for thirty years.

But I do know this: blithely allowing this terrible stripping to occur is a blot on the conscience of America, and especially on the conscience of the church. If we as believers choose to forget that everyone—even the shrunken soul lying in the doorway—is made in the image of God, can we say we know our Creator? If we respond to others based on their outward appearance, haven't we entirely missed the point of the gospel?

Christ cared a lot about the simple dignities. He stopped to talk to lepers, and touch them with healing (Luke 5:13). He prepared meals for strangers. He rescued outcasts. He wept with those who wept.

Of course, the issue isn't completely defined by our response. The consequences of substance abuse, poverty, and irresponsibility have left countless men and women on our streets without a single outward shred of dignity. But Christ is not deterred by that. As C. S. Lewis wrote: "Christ died for men precisely because men are not worth dying for: to make them worth it."

103

To me, one of the best things about the gospel is that Jesus Christ proclaims and restores human and eternal worth for *everyone who believes*—regardless of what a person might look or smell like now, no matter what's crawling through his hair.

And because we follow this Christ, each of us has both the ability and the responsibility ("response-ability") to do the same.

CHURCH LOCK DOWN

Early on a Friday evening, just after the sun had set, Sam and I were walking from the library back down to the Portland waterfront where we had decided the Friday night crowd would offer a prime panhandling opportunity. We didn't say much as we walked until we passed a church.

"Oh, my gosh!" I exclaimed, stopping. "You've got to be kidding me."

"What?" said Sam. Then he saw what I was looking at. "Oh," he murmured.

A large gray church rose up behind a wrought iron fence in front of us. The building was old and weathered. Above the mahogany double doors hung a sign in red letters: *"No Trespassing. Church Business Only."* A new chain and two huge padlocks secured the gate at the sidewalk.

"It would take bolt cutters and a battering ram to get into that church," I said, suddenly angry. "'Come to me all you who are weary and heavy laden'? Yeah, and what, die on my front steps?"

We turned to keep walking toward the waterfront. Sure, a church needs to protect its property, but what we had just seen seemed excessive, and sent a negative, uncaring message.

Sam was having the same thoughts. "Let's say your life is

falling apart and you need help. Would you want to go there?"

"Nope," I said. "Anywhere *but* there. But the world *is* the church's business—and that's exactly who they're shutting out!"

"Correct me if I'm wrong," said Sam, "But aren't the people in a sanctuary a whole lot more important than the sanctuary itself?"

We walked past a market that sold pop, beer, wine, cigarettes, pornography. The doors were wedged open. Ragged people came and went.

It was one of the places that never close.

THE STUPID, SMALL THINGS

By the end of our time in Portland, Sam and I had been with one another twenty-four hours a day, seven days a week for nearly two months. Tensions were running high.

Imagine taking two twenty-something guys, both strong-minded, both liking to be in charge, both prideful, both amazingly confident in their own ways of doing things. Take these two and put them under huge stress. More exactly, shove them out on the streets together where, as companions in mutual misery, they must depend on each other constantly for support, accountability, understanding, friendship, and mercy…for weeks.

What happens sooner or later?

Meltdown.

As you might expect, it was the stupid, small things that set us off. Early one evening we walked out of the downtown library to get a meal at a local soup kitchen. At the bottom of the library stairs, I turned left. Sam turned right. Either direction would have eventually gotten us where we needed to go.

After a couple of steps we both noticed the other was missing and stopped to see what had happened. There we stood, about ten feet apart, astonished at the other person's ridiculous choice.

"Where you going?" Sam asked. He was holding up his hands in utter amazement.

"Where am I going?" I said sarcastically. "Where are *you* going?"

"Well, I'm going to get some food, buddy."

"Well, so am I—*buddy!*"

"So?"

"What do you mean, *so*? Are you some kind of moron?"

Forget maturity, patience, humility. Trying circumstances have a way of destroying all that. For several minutes, while Portland city life flowed by us, we stood there on the sidewalk going at it like three-year-olds. Neither of us was willing to budge an inch.

Why would you, when the other guy is obviously insane?

- - -

A couple hours later we were lying on our backs in our usual sleeping spot near the Willamette. Stars shone dimly through high clouds. We were talking, but the conversation was not going well, either. We were arguing one of the finer points of Christian doctrine—the faith/works question: Can a person be saved with no good works to show for it or will genuine salvation always show itself in good works? (Of course, some of the greatest minds in history have debated this one—I can't really remember why we thought two pinheads under a bridge would get anywhere on it.)

As things heated up, I felt my grip on faith tightening while my passion for good works loosened. Actually, I wanted to knock Sam's teeth out.

Sam wasn't doing much better. At one point, he looked away in frustration before turning to face me. Then he let fly with a thundering left hook, spiritually speaking.

"You should pray about that, Mike," he said fervently.

What a cheap shot! I couldn't believe it! Like praying about this would bring me around to his ridiculous point of view? I thought he was brainless and told him so.

I was beginning to wonder if the truth that two are better than one might not apply in this instance. Okay, originally I'd felt tremendous relief when Sam agreed to become my traveling partner (so did my family and advisers). But that was then. At this point in our journey, on this night, by this river—I just wasn't having that feeling anymore. Two may be better than one in a general, mathematical sense. But when you're stuck with one guy for weeks trying to scavenge a life—and the diet has obviously killed off that guy's common sense—it's a recipe for unmitigated disaster. And we were doing our best to have one.

Before long we were both sitting up in our bags, hands waving in the night, dredging up every random frustration we could think of and lobbing it at the other person. We went from specific, to general, to extremely general. For my part, I went from not liking Sam's point of view, to not liking sleeping in a stinking bag next to Sam by this or any river, to just not liking Sam. Sam was the problem; the problem was Sam—end of argument. (The rush of clarity I experienced when I arrived at that conclusion was absolutely invigorating.)

Of course, the conversation went nowhere. Finally we agreed to go to sleep and finish our "discussion" in the morning.

107

But wouldn't you know it, when we woke up, we went right back at it. After more insults and accusations and stubbornness and anger, we were ready to happily murder one another (in the name of God, of course).

Foolish, don't you think?

But then a glimmer of wisdom broke through. Sam and I agreed to take a couple of hours apart. He went for a walk, and I stayed behind under the bridge with the bags.

- - -

While Sam was gone I spent some time reading and praying. I was skimming through Colossians, still trying, I'll admit, to find Scriptures to prove that I was right and Sam was wrong. But Paul's words stopped me in my tracks:

> *Therefore, as God's chosen people, holy and dearly loved, clothe yourselves with compassion, kindness, humility, gentleness and patience. Bear with each other and forgive whatever grievances you may have against one another. Forgive as the Lord forgave you. And over all these virtues put on love, which binds them all together in perfect unity.* (Colossians 3:12–14)

I felt the Spirit dropping the truth into my heart one word at a time—compassion, kindness, humility, gentleness, and patience. Almost nothing I had thought, felt, or said in the previous twenty-four hours could be described in those terms.

How had my genuine affection and admiration for Sam given way to such complete frustration? By holding adamantly to my own notions of the "correct way" to believe and behave, I decided. Sam and I were doing exactly what Paul said not to.

A couple of hours later, Sam returned. By then, we had each cooled off and could finally just talk.

Interestingly, in our time of separate reflection, God had shown both of us the same thing—that we needed each other and that unity between us was a big deal. Making room for disagreement, and any friction that might go with it, was far better than the alternative: going it alone on the streets.

We agreed on something else: to put unity firmly in the "works" column. We decided that the idea of unity just wasn't going to be good enough. You can't survive with just an idea. It won't keep you safe. You can't eat it. You can't even give it away.

We decided that, for us, real unity should be something we could see and feel, something we could lean on even when frustrations ran high. Especially then, we decided. And only then would two *actually* be better than one.

Things went better after that for Sam and me. Sure, we still had disagreements, but fewer of the stupid, small ones. We discovered we could work things out most of the time. And when we couldn't, there was always a nice, long, solo walk to take.

UNEXPECTED GRACE

A few nights after our big blowup, I rolled over in my sleeping bag and opened my eyes. Slowly the world came back into my awareness: the concrete, the trash piled near the concrete supports, the smell of urine. The whole view was sepia colored beneath the city light burning close by. Sam and I were back under the Hawthorne Bridge after having escaped yet another Portland downpour earlier that evening.

What had woken me?

I fumbled for my glasses, sat up, and looked around. Everything seemed to be in order—Sam was there, a few feet away; both our packs were accounted for, and our guitars. What was it, then?

I sat there for a few seconds, blinking and rubbing the sleep from my eyes before slipping from my sleeping bag and walking quietly from under the bridge. I stretched for a moment and rubbed a spot on my hip that had grown tender from lying on the concrete. Though the clouds still hung close to the city, the rain had stopped and it was a cool, pleasant evening. I made my way to one of the nearby benches and sat down to watch the city lights playing on the dark water of the Willamette River. For several seconds the only sound I heard was the murmur of the river flowing past.

110

And then I heard what had woken me.

A long, clear note came over the surface of the dark and chaotic water, filling the night air around me. At first I thought it was the horn of a small boat somewhere on the river. But then it changed, gaining in pitch for a moment before climbing another note higher and dropping down again.

I stood from my bench and walked toward the river, looking to my right for the source of the music. There, next to the river on a concrete outcropping a few hundred feet from me, was the dark outline of an old man hunched over a trumpet. The sound continued over the river, reaching me and stealing my breath.

He was playing "Amazing Grace."

I fought back tears for a moment or two before finally giving in. Why not? He played and played, putting more energy into every note as the song progressed. I would have sung along if I could have, but mouthing the words was all I could do through my tears.

It was the lyrics of the third verse that really got me:

Through many dangers, toils, and snares
we have already come.
'Twas grace that brought us safe thus far,
and grace will lead us home.

At the end of that verse, I plopped myself down right there on the concrete and wept. I wept with thankfulness for God's protection thus far in the journey that Sam and I were on. I wept with a yearning for home, for friends, and for family. I wept for the people we had met and the need for God's amazing grace amid all the ruptured relationships, smashed dreams, and broken lives. I wept with a longing for final redemption—for the ills of our lives and our cities and our world to be mended, for the broken to be made whole, for the lonely to be comforted, for the dead to come to life.

I guess our journey was beginning to take its toll on me. I wept and wept.

At last the old trumpeter finished his song, and slowly I ran out of tears.

As I sat there trying to catch my breath, an unexpected and inexplicable peace took root deep within me. I knew that we (the two of us—and the whole human race for that matter) are not alone. Despite all the indications to the contrary, we are not adrift on a shoreless sea of human need and misery. There is hope—hope of an approaching wholeness and redemption. The Lord has come to us and is coming still. Coming over the dark and chaotic mess of our world, all the more breathtaking in the unexpected ways He makes Himself known.

"We hear a Christian assure someone that he will 'pray over' his problem, knowing full well that he intends to use prayer as a substitute for service. It is much easier to pray that a poor friend's needs may be supplied than to supply them."

A. W. TOZER, OF GOD AND MEN

Start: September 3rd, 2003
End: September 28th, 2003
Duration: 26 days
Locations: Tenderloin District, Golden Gate Park, Berkeley

bbie Hoffman, a noted radical leftist of the 60s, once proclaimed in a speech in San Francisco, "The big battles that we won cannot be reversed." In no city did his statement seem truer. The streets of San Francisco—where free love and recreational drugs got their start—are now crowded with fifteen thousand loveless, drug-addicted homeless people.

Although San Francisco's Haight-Ashbury district was at the center of Hoffman's "all you need is love" subculture, we didn't find much love there either. For example, the gang fight

I describe at the beginning of this book took place in Golden Gate Park, right next to the Haight. In most ways, San Francisco was the most difficult environment we encountered. Cold, wet, windy, foggy nights; hours of panhandling without earning a dime; standing in long lines at feeding kitchens; interracial hatred. It all went together to make our month in the City by the Bay extremely draining—physically, mentally, emotionally, and spiritually.

After a week of trying to beat the crowds in the downtown Tenderloin District, we moved out to Golden Gate Park. We spent many nights sleeping in the park across from St. Mary's Medical Center. Around the park, we faced schizophrenics and gang fights, but at least we weren't trying to compete for spare change with the thousands of other homeless who are permanently camped in the Tenderloin.

There were glimpses of hope, though. Several times, God provided wonderful meals through others, some of whom we never even met. And we encountered three amazing Christians who were putting their faith into action by blessing people on the streets. They did simple stuff, like handing out pizza in Jesus' name. But it helped. They reminded Sam and me that no matter what we faced, like John 1 says, the Light has not been overcome by the darkness.

IN THE PRESENCE OF MY ENEMIES

Trying to live off the streets in the heart of downtown San Francisco almost did us in. Panhandling on crowded corners and in subway stations proved exhausting and almost pointless. Our guitar cases stayed as empty as our stomachs. The subway tunnels felt like tombs—plenty of bodies but no life.

We felt invisible, disdained, and increasingly unable to earn even enough for the cheapest burger. At every turn, we felt opposed and pressed back by enemies—seen and unseen.

After about a week we were sinking into despair.

One midday, walking through the Tenderloin, we came upon a lineup of hundreds of shabby people waiting in a dark side street to eat at St. Anthony's, a large feeding kitchen. The scene did nothing to cheer us up. The street itself was strewn with trash, the wall behind the line was puke-stained, and the crowd reeked of body odor and alcohol. Off to one side, an old man with one shoe paced back and forth toting a ragged cardboard box and mumbling quietly to himself. It looked like a scene from an apocalyptic movie—the kind where the world as we know it has ended, but somehow a desperate, hungry horde has found a place that still has food.

Well, we were shabby, desperate, and hungry, too. So why not join the horde?

We stepped into line behind a guy with short blond hair, wearing a colorful jacket that was badly torn and much too small for him. When he heard me cough, he turned around in alarm. A large silver feather earring dangling from his left ear swung violently from his quick movement.

"What's your name?" he asked a little too intensely. An odd, nervous smile showed rows of dead and dying teeth.

"Mike," I said. "Yours?"

"Chris," he said, glancing quickly to his left and his right. "You new here?" He was still smiling oddly.

"Yes," I answered, cautiously. "Why do you ask?"

Chris answered in hushed tones. "Don't go past Mission to the south after two in the morning. The Latinos hang out there. They'll kill you just because you're white. You'd be sur-

prised how easy it is to make a person disappear in this city."
As he talked, Chris looked around furtively.

"Oh, really," said Sam, interested but uncomfortable.
"Anywhere else we shouldn't go?"

"Yeah," Chris said wide-eyed. "Don't go any further down
Market after midnight. The blacks hang out there. They'll kill
you just because you're white, too."

A person behind us cursed and Chris realized the line
ahead of him had moved. He turned to catch up, his earring
glinting in the afternoon sun.

"I don't think he's kidding," Sam said in low tones.

"Nope," I said grimly. I noticed a dark glob of phlegm on
my guitar case. Disgusted, I scraped the case along the wall as
I walked, trying to get rid of the mess. I got rid of it alright, but
wore a nasty hole in the case lining in the process.

"Let's leave tomorrow!" I said to Sam when I'd caught up
to him. "We'll play in the subway again tomorrow morning,
then take the bus out to Golden Gate Park and Haight Street,
like we'd planned."

Sam nodded. "You read my mind."

- - -

The next day we made a mistake and got off the bus two
miles before our destination. That left a lot of walking, and we
were already feeling low.

To match our moods, the afternoon was gloomy, a pale light
shining through the thick fog that had rolled in off the Pacific.

Most people think of fog as peaceful and soothing. But
when you're living in it day after day—and things aren't going
well to boot—fog can feel downright malicious. It presses you

down in the half-light. It invades everything with moisture. It bites with cold. Relentlessly, it wears you down.

That afternoon, a light drizzle started. Fog *and* rain? Not what I needed. The fog and drizzle collected on my glasses in a mass of droplets. As we trudged uphill, the weight of our gear growing with every step, the world I looked out on kept dividing and smearing. Every now and then a drop would streak down my glasses, leaving a brief window of clarity, then the wet blur would close in again.

When twenty minutes of walking had left us soaked through by rain and perspiration, we came upon a coffee shop. An older man standing atop a ladder by the windows yelled a hello to us as we neared. That seemed downright inviting, so we ducked inside, found a corner table, and set down our packs and guitars. Pleasant jazz played on the radio while comfortable chairs and couches called out to our sore bodies.

117

The shop turned out to be a restaurant as well. The air was filled with the aroma of fresh ground coffee and pancake batter on the grill. Not that we could buy anything. Our last meal had been lunch the day before at Anthony's. The panhandling that morning had proved fruitless yet again, and after buying bus passes we were broke.

Huge platters of pancakes—spread with bananas, butter, Nutella, and maple syrup—arrived to the only other customers in the place, a young couple in hiking boots and new Gore-Tex rain jackets. They seemed to approve of the pancakes, which were the most glorious culinary creations I'd ever seen. But they obviously didn't approve of us. They leaned together, talking in hushed tones while they took a few bites.

But only a few. Then they rose, grabbed their rain jackets, and departed.

What to say? I guess the wet stink of Sam and me had overpowered those wonderful aromas coming from the kitchen. We felt embarrassed and regretful that we'd chased them out. Well, not *too* regretful, because now we couldn't take our eyes off the delicious spread on their recently vacated table.

"Excellent," Sam said, looking hopeful.

"You up for it?" I asked.

"You bet!" he said excitedly, slamming his hands on our own empty table in emphasis.

We jumped up to walk over to the table. "Do you mind if we eat the rest of this?" I asked the girl behind the counter, hoping my excitement and good manners would make up for our unpleasant presence.

"Sure. Go ahead," she said with a smile, and walked into the kitchen without looking back. Ecstatic, we picked up the platters heaped with the most perfect pancakes I'd ever seen (even with a bite or two missing) and took them back to our seats.

After an elated prayer of thanks—I think it was the most joyous prayer of our whole time in San Francisco—we feasted. The dark canyons of the Tenderloin seemed far away. The crazies, the lines of defeated and hungry people, the uncaring commuters seemed far away, too. Even the fog seemed far away. All that was near was the sweet and surprising goodness of God.

When we were finally finished, we sat back to digest.

"You believe that?" I asked.

"No, I don't," said Sam. "That was *so* good! I can't believe they left all this for us."

That wonderful meal went a long way toward mending our bodies and our spirits after the harshness of life downtown.

118

"In the presence of my enemies," the psalmist wrote, "You spread a table heaping with pancakes before me."

Or something like that.

BED FOR THE NIGHT

A bitter wind whipped down the street, carrying a swirl of trash along with it. I sank deeper into my sweatshirt, which did little against the cold.

Sam and I had decided to come downtown to try to score a bed at a shelter, and we were waiting in line along with two hundred other men and women. Anyone who wanted to get a bed had to line up at three in the afternoon outside the offices of the organization that coordinated all shelter beds in San Francisco.

It was a long wait. Shuffling forward in line an inch at a time is no way to keep warm.

Finally, we got to the door.

"Next!" a man shouted.

Once inside, we went to the counter, gave our social security numbers, and had our fingerprints scanned into the system. "Line up outside again at five-thirty tonight and we'll get you your beds," the man behind the counter droned.

"Next!"

Sam and I walked back out into the cold.

By this time it was a quarter of four, and we didn't have enough time to go anywhere without risking losing our shot at a bed. So we decided to just hang around.

More waiting.

By five-thirty, the wind had picked up even more, and the crowd had swelled to about four hundred. Sam and I shuffled over to join the ranks, trying to use our backpacks to shield us from the wind. The line began to move rapidly forward as an army of passenger vans from various shelters hauled away their human cargo.

But just as our turn came, the line stopped, and a woman emerged from the building with a clipboard in hand.

"May I have your attention please," she said. Conversation around us stopped, all eyes directed anxiously toward her. "Unfortunately for you folks, everybody's full tonight. There aren't any more beds. Sorry."

With a nod, she walked back inside, closed the door, and threw the bolt lock.

The old man in front of us coughed. "Gonna freeze tonight," he said, then he turned and limped away. The rest of the men and women melted away without comment. Apparently they were used to the routine: Wait in the cold for a bed. Wait in the cold for no bed.

For a few minutes, Sam and I were too discouraged to speak. Finally, Sam asked, "Where to now?"

"What do you say we go back to Haight?" I suggested. "We could panhandle a little, then sleep by St. Mary's again?"

"Sounds good to me."

The nice thing about buying a fare on most urban bus systems is that you get a transfer that's good for about an hour. The bad thing about standing in a line for four hours and not getting a bed is that your transfer is no longer valid. And Sam and I were completely broke.

We decided to be "entrepreneurial"—you know, make an opportunity where none exists. We jumped on the next bus going toward Golden Gate Park, and holding up our expired transfers, rushed by the driver hoping he wouldn't oust us. He didn't.

That night, after panhandling unsuccessfully on the Haight for a while, we packed up and walked toward St. Mary's. Along the way, we passed a small Indian restaurant. In the planter out in front we spied two take-out plastic containers. Hopefully, we grabbed both containers to see what might await us. They were full of food! With a yell of excitement, we sat down on the spot to eat.

Ah, dinner! It was a mouth-watering meal of rice, couscous, and curried chicken, apparently put out as charity when the restaurant closed. God had fed us again—this time by keeping a feast safely in a planter till we could show up to eat it. We were grateful and encouraged.

When we had finished eating, we pushed on toward St. Mary's in thick fog.

"Good thing we've walked this way so many times before," I said.

"Yeah, it'd be tough to find otherwise," said Sam.

"Good thing we walked by the restaurant."

"Yeah! Blessings come when you least expect them."

We arrived at our usual spot across from the hospital, the bright St. Mary's sign glowing in the fog. As I spread out my sleeping bag, Sam left to use the restroom at the hospital. I sat on the picnic table journaling by the streetlight until Sam returned. When he came back, I took my turn using the facilities.

By the time I returned Sam was buried deep in his bag. I crawled into my own, surprised at how comforting a three-dollar thrift store sleeping bag could feel if the circumstances were right.

Sam and I prayed aloud up into the fog and fell asleep.

About two in the morning, a violent gust of ocean air

blew through the trees above us, shaking off huge drops of moisture and sending them cascading down on us.

"Is it raining?" Sam asked groggily.

"Nah, it's just the trees," I said, and pulled myself further into my bed for the night.

WAKE-UP CALL

I can still hear that obnoxious refrain crowding its way into my dreams. Whoever was calling me was having fun. His voice started high, dipped low, then rose again in complete mockery.

"G-O-O-o-d m-o-r-n-I-N-G!"

He obviously liked the effect because he repeated it.

"G-O-O-o-d m-o-r-n-I-N-G!"

And repeated it again.

In my dream, I grabbed my alarm clock and hurled it against the far wall, where it shattered into a thousand tiny pieces. That felt good.

The voice rang out again.

Finally coming to, I sat up in my bag. Leaves and twigs that had drifted onto me as I slept slid off. Sam sat up, too. I fumbled for my glasses, wiped off the condensation, and looked around.

A man in a business suit stood beyond throwing distance but close enough for effect. He held a steaming latte and a *Wall Street Journal*, and was attached by a blue leash to a bored dog. And now that the guy saw he had our attention, he called out yet again, "G-O-O-o-d m-o-r-n-I-N-G!"

"Uh, good morning?" I answered.

"Now that I have your attention—you aren't supposed to be here," he said brightly. Then, careful not to spill his latte, he pointed across the street to the posh buildings. "You see all those apartments over there?"

"Yeah, we see them," said Sam.

"Good! Now imagine you work hard six days a week to live there and every morning you open your blinds to look out onto beautiful Golden Gate Park." His voice was rising to a yell as he spoke. "Do you really think we want to see *you* sleeping here? Leave *now*—before I call the police!"

With that, he turned and walked away. Only then did I notice that his dog had only three legs. Its pathetic hopping cut quite a contrast to the businessman's arrogant stride.

"There is *so* much I could say right now!" I sputtered.

"About the man or his three-legged dog?" asked Sam.

"You just don't want to know…!"

"Let's go get some coffee," said Sam, trying to cheer me up. "I can smell McDonald's from here."

123

- - -

It had been a tough day in the Tenderloin. We'd spent hours playing in the subway, with little success. We'd even split up, taking either end of a long underground corridor, hoping to double our take, but hadn't done any better. When evening came, we were more than ready to pack it in.

Sam mentioned seeing a courtyard that might work well for the night.

"Sounds good," I said, and we picked up our gear and set off down the long corridor toward the exit. When we reached the exit where I'd been playing only minutes earlier, two other homeless men had gathered and were both playing guitars. The open case in front of them already had four dollars crumpled up in it. "Guess we're just not good enough!" I said to Sam, pointing at the case.

We walked up a couple of steps to the courtyard. It was level, reasonably quiet, and well protected from the wind. I laughed.

"What?" Sam asked, curious.

"You know," I said, "if our circumstances were different I would tell you this courtyard is a perfect place to sit with your girlfriend on a pleasant San Francisco evening. Now, I'm thinking it's a perfect place to sleep for a whole chilly night."

Sam agreed on the perspective thing. He said he'd spied a perfect sleeping corner next to the city library yesterday. "There was a security camera, but I figured if we moved quickly enough we could get there and get set up without being noticed. So I'm at the library, but I'm thinking about where to sleep—not books."

"That's what I'm talking about!" I said, laughing.

"Do you think we'll ever go back to seeing things like we used to?" asked Sam.

"Probably not," I said. "I mean, there will come a time when we are not wondering where we'll be sleeping for the night. But I think we'll always remember what it was like to have to think like we do now. At least I hope so."

We stretched out our sleeping bags near a replica of a trolley car that had been turned into a café but was locked up for the night. Just as I was turning in, I noticed a couple of large planters on the retaining wall above us with several sprinkler heads showing. "Let's pray those sprinklers don't come on while we're trying to sleep," I said, not even wanting to think about the scene.

"Yeah," Sam said. "We don't need a shower for at least another week."

124

At about three in the morning though, we woke under a sudden torrent of water. We were in such a hurry to get out of our bags and escape the drenching, we kept tripping and falling. The water reeked strangely of chemicals and burned our eyes. In seconds, we were soaked.

But when we finally got clear, we saw that it wasn't sprinklers doing the damage. A small man with a white hard hat was peering over the balcony above us, holding a fire hose. He began yelling in a language we couldn't understand, motioning for us to leave. When we hesitated, he motioned threateningly with his huge hose.

"Can you understand him?" Sam asked.

"Sure can!" I exclaimed. "And I don't want another blast from that thing!"

There was nothing to do but pick up our soggy belongings and start looking for somewhere else to endure the rest of the night.

"He's cleaning off the streets," Sam said, as we sloshed our way along. "All the street trash is getting washed away. Cigarette butts, newspapers, bird doo, and us. Away we go!" He sounded mournful.

"Come on, bud," I said, less frustrated now that we were up and moving. "Think of it as a homeless person's alarm clock."

YOU JUST KNOW IT'S DARK IN THERE

The struggle to survive on the street is demanding enough for the alcoholics and addicts, but for some it's unimaginably worse. As Richard White Jr. notes, "Most of the homeless we see in our downtown business districts, parks, and other public places are seriously mentally ill."

Many of the people Sam and I hung around with were clearly suffering from some form of mental disorder—from bipolar disorder to severe chronic depression to schizophrenia. Some didn't seem to have definite diagnosis to explain what went on in their private mental hells. But on the streets, that didn't really matter. You just know it's dark in there.

One early morning, Sam and I were walking across Golden Gate Park toward McDonald's for breakfast. We had slept at our normal spot the previous evening, directly across from St. Mary's Hospital. Except for a police car that had driven slowly past twice while Sam and I sat journaling on a picnic table, it had been an uneventful evening.

St. Mary's had become a home base of sorts; it held the only twenty-four-hour bathroom we could find in that area. On alternate evenings, there was a particular security guard who had befriended us. He let us use the facilities, no questions asked. One of us would stay in the park with guitars and packs while the other used the bathrooms. The arrangement worked better than going without water or having to use a tree in the park.

That morning as we neared McDonald's an older transient came walking past. When he saw the Bible Sam was carrying, he pointed to Sam and shouted, "The Bible is untrue! Un...true!"

Curious, Sam and I stopped to talk. Surprisingly, we were able to have a real conversation with him, at least for a while. After chatting about the park, the weather, the feeding kitchens, and the price of burgers at McDonald's, we asked why he thought the Bible was untrue. He mumbled something about Sam's Bible being the wrong version.

126

"I'm not sure the version matters a lot," Sam said. "The important question is whether you know Jesus Christ."

The man looked away for a moment, thinking. Then he looked back at Sam and said intently, "Yes, I know Jesus Christ. He is the forgiver of my sins, the only hope I have. Son of the Almighty God, Creator of the Universe—I believe in Him alone."

That wasn't the response Sam and I had been expecting. But the old man wasn't finished. With his demeanor shifting to fury he leaned forward and stared into me intently for a moment before turning his face to Sam's. Then he screamed, "I *am* Jesus Christ!"

He tore his gaze away from us and started walking down the sidewalk, away from McDonald's.

We watched him go, mumbling to himself.

"Huh," I said, looking at Sam.

"That sucked," he said.

We continued on toward McDonald's, deep in thought. Sam started talking about a vacation Bible school he'd been part of once where a man with a long beard played Jesus. "The kids loved it," he said. "The guy was just like all the pictures they had seen. After the skit had ended a little girl came up to me and grabbed my hand. When I bent down to talk with her she threw her arms around me. After the hug she pulled back and looked me right in the eyes. 'I'm so glad Jesus has come to visit our city,' she said. Before I could try to explain to her that the guy wasn't *actually* Jesus, she hugged me again and ran off."

We tried to figure out what "whoever believes in his heart and confesses with his mouth that Jesus is Lord" would mean in cases where the person doing the believing was

127

clearly confused. What would it mean for our friend who said he believes in Jesus Christ as the only hope for his salvation, but he also believes that he is Jesus Christ?

We didn't have too many handy answers. Except that God's love for all His children is beyond our understanding, and that "the Lord knows those who are his" (2 Timothy 2:19).

- - -

Of all the mental disorders common to the streets, schizophrenia is the most disquieting to watch, and though our months in Denver, D.C., and Portland had led to many meetings with such men and women, nothing could have prepared us for our encounters with Henry.

Sam and I sat at the mouth to Golden Gate Park late one evening, fog swirling through the tree tops. The evening was actually peaceful, a rarity on the streets. The cluster of street people around us was taken up with a game of quarters, a seemingly endless way to pass time. Quite a few of the gamers were drinking heavily or smoking pot, or both.

Suddenly the conversations and laughter quieted as everyone's attention was drawn toward a man who was crossing the street. As soon as his foot stepped into the park, every dog in the courtyard began barking viciously, ears back, hair raised, fangs bared. Next to Sam and me a massive pit bull lunged against a short rope that was being restrained with difficulty by his large owner. That moment still haunts me.

What made the moment so eerie was that every dog had immediately *sensed* this man's presence, not from merely seeing him or smelling him or hearing him. Simply by his *presence* they were transformed into aggressive beasts. Several dogs escaped their leashes and began biting the man's hands and tearing at his jeans. It took several people to pull them off. We learned from the others that the man's name was Henry.

Henry's movements and demeanor were unnerving. He was constantly moving, rolling his eyes, rolling his head around on his neck, swinging his arms wildly, spinning around in circles and yelling. Marco, the man who had started the brawl two nights earlier, was the only one to show him any kindness or friendship, and Henry actually calmed a little as they stood talking.

A few nights later in a nearby McDonald's we saw Henry again when he came to use the restroom. After he emerged, his movements still as erratic and uncontrolled as they had been the night in the park, we called him over to our table and offered him two of the ninety-nine-cent hamburgers we had just bought with some of our evening's panhandling money. He readily accepted them and sat down two tables away to eat. It was hard to watch. Chunks of his burger fell out onto the table as he ate, rocking back and forth, yelling now and then as he chewed.

I am not comfortable saying that Henry was demon possessed. I don't know. I will say that the experiences surrounding him were some of the most challenging for me to deal with or explain. How did every dog in the park *sense* his presence? Why were his actions so uncontrolled and erratic?

In his book *This Present Darkness,* Frank Perretti writes a scene in which a demon sits on top of a car hood while a woman inside tries desperately to start her vehicle. I know we live in a world in which there is more going on than meets the eye. And we fight against more than the powers of this world. Yet I prefer to live in a world I can explain, so I tend to lean away from blaming disagreeable things in life on demonic influence. I heard once of someone praying over his toothbrush because he had gotten a cavity and blamed it on a demon. I say, stop praying and start brushing, but that's just me.

The last time we saw Henry was the day before we left San Francisco for Phoenix as he was stumbling through the center of the park, talking frantically to himself, shaking his fists wildly at the sky. All I could think about was the fact that Jesus spent time with people just like Henry. Jesus came to them, healed them, cast the demons out of them—gave them life and peace.

But here's the thing: Jesus expects us to reach out to Henrys, too—and He draws the expectation in the clearest of terms. How we treat people in this life will determine whether we hear "whatever you did for one of the least of these…you did for me" (Matthew 25:40) or "whatever you *did not* do for one of the least of these, *you did not do for me*" (Matthew 25:45, emphasis added).

Ultimately, it doesn't matter whether Henry or the man who thinks he's Jesus are clinically diagnosed as mentally ill or spiritually described as demon possessed. Neither label gets us off the hook of what *we* are called to do and be in their lives.

THE OTHER JESUS GUY

The four-inch gash across Link's forehead was evidence of Marco's displeasure. (You remember Marco, the guy who started the bloody brawl I described in chapter 1.)

The day before, Marco had unleashed more violence, this time beating Link with a three-foot lead pipe. Even though Link was more than twice Marco's size, he had suffered terribly while other park people watched. This end of Golden Gate Park was Marco's domain. No one questioned his "justice," not even Link.

Tonight, Sam and I were back in the park, sitting in a circle that included both men. What brought the group together this night was Link's bottle of whiskey, which was making the rounds. Link was already well under the influence, but when the whiskey came by he was ready for more.

Lifting the bottle, he said somberly, "This is for my brother who died two days ago when somebody stabbed him in the stomach."

He poured out a few drops on the concrete, then tilted his head back and took a long drink. Everyone in the circle nodded silently. Toasting street family members who had died was an important drinking ritual here.

When he put the bottle down, Link's face was streaming with tears. He offered the bottle to us, but we declined. Earlier we had passed on an offer of a bong. Even in his blurry state, Link seemed to notice.

131

"Do you now th' other Jesus guy?" he asked.

"Who, him?" I replied, pointing to Sam.

"No, the *other* Jesus guy!?"

"What other Jesus guy?" I asked. Maybe this conversation would take his mind off of his brother.

"You know, th' other guy who doesn' drink or get high." Link was slurring. "He comes roun' here. Brings pizza, hamburgers…"

Another guy in the circle piped in. "That guy's awesome!"

We said we hadn't met him. "But I'd sure love to," Sam said. "When does he usually come around?"

"How should I know?" Link mumbled, then he got up and stumbled away.

- - -

The next evening, just before Sam and I left the park to pan-handle, the "other Jesus guy" arrived. We saw him parking a small car across the street. When he called out to a few park people, they cheered and shuffled over, returning with twelve boxes of pizza. While a group gathered to chow down, "the other Jesus guy" joined us.

"I'm George," he said. "Are you guys new around here? I don't remember seeing you before."

"Yeah," Sam said, "We're just sort of passing through."

"We came in on the Greyhound about two weeks ago from Portland, but we were in the Tenderloin for a while," I added.

"Wow!" George said, eyebrows raised. "Tough place!"

Later, when the pizza was gone and the three of us were walking the empty boxes to a dumpster, we had a chance to talk more. I asked George why he came to the park.

"What do you mean?" George looked confused.

"The pizza, hanging out down here, being nice to the people no one else cares about. All of it. Why?"

"I figure they're hungry, and hey, everybody likes pizza, right?" said George. But he looked uncomfortable with the question.

"That's the easy answer," said Sam. "What's the *real* reason?"

"Okay," George said, realizing we were serious. "You really want to know? I do this because my faith tells me to. The Bible clearly says, if you see someone hungry, feed them; if you see someone naked, clothe them. Those words weren't written for us to make books and sermons about. They're written so people don't go hungry and naked. And they require action from all followers of Christ, not just the rescue missions. Anyway, that's how I see it. So I'm trying to live my life that way and be pleasing to Jesus."

"Whew!" I said, inspired.

"Do you know what they call you around here?" Sam asked. "The Jesus Guy."

"Highest compliment I could ever receive," George said with a big smile. "But you know what? I've never once come down here and preached. At least not in the typical fashion— you know, with yelling and Bible thumping."

Sam and I took a few minutes to tell George about ourselves, and that we shared his faith. We thanked him for his powerful witness for Christ in the park.

"Isn't it amazing," I said, "that when we live as we're called and do what we're commanded, the gospel *does* get preached— one way or another?"

"I think so," said George. He was scanning the park. There were the usual strollers and losers and drunks and punks, the usual American riffraff. But George was looking the place over like he owned it, like it was his own backyard. "Live as you're called, and the good news will go forth. I like that."

"Remember that the poor are people with names," writes Bryant Myers, author of *Walking with the Poor.* "[They are] people with whom and among whom God has been working before we even knew they were there."

For Sam and me, George was proof that God was at work in Golden Gate Park. The rest of the evening, instead of feeling oppressed by the violence, cursing, and drunkenness all around us, we felt the presence of Christ. One of His disciples was actually invading this brutal corner of the world with the

133

good news. We prayed that one day soon Link and Marco and the others would open up and take it in.

THE GRACE OF PIZZA

It was a busy Saturday night in Berkeley, throngs of students everywhere. We'd come here on BART (the Bay Area Rapid Transit system) earlier in the day in search of better panhandling. So far, we were doing okay on the donations, not so great on the requests. We just never seemed to know the songs others wanted to hear.

My fingers were getting sore from hours of playing. I stood to stretch, then yawned and laughed.

"What?" Sam asked.

"You know, before we came out here, a part of me was excited to have all this time to play the guitar. I figured I'd get a lot better. Six months on the street and I'd be the next Dave Matthews."

Sam confessed to having similar thoughts.

I examined the calluses on my left hand. "We've gotten a *little* better, but not much. Out here, you don't play to get better, you play to eat."

"Yup, and that means being heard above the traffic."

"So we're not really playing and singing, right?" I said. "We're strumming and yelling. We're getting better at strumming and yelling."

We both laughed, and I sat down to begin again. Just then three guys walked past, the lead guy carrying a pizza box.

"Hey, bro!" I called. "You going to eat the rest of that pizza?"

The guy stopped, looked from Sam and me to his box of pizza, then said, "Nope." Shaking his head, he walked over.

"You want it?" he asked.

"Sure!" I said, and he handed it down to us.

We thanked him profusely. "No problem," he said, walking away. "Enjoy."

Opening the box we found half a pepperoni pizza. "Unbelievable!" Sam yelled.

"This is the good stuff!" I said, grabbing a piece. "Father, thank You for this food!"

We sat there, happily devouring the still-warm pizza. By the time we were down to the crumbs, we were ready for more conversation.

"'Father, thank You for this food' means something different out here, doesn't it?" I said.

"Sure does," said Sam. "I don't know if I'll ever say it so sincerely again after we get back."

"I hope I don't change," I said.

135

We sat watching people walk by, thinking about pizza and thankfulness. "What do you think would have happened if the Israelites hadn't gone out and picked up the manna God sent?" I asked.

"And your meaning is?" said Sam.

"I mean, don't you think they would have starved if they never actually went out and picked the manna off the ground?"

Sam looked at me as if I had pepperoni poisoning. Finally, he responded. "Yeah, probably. They had to eat, and God *was* providing, but—yes—they had to go out and pick it up."

"Exactly!" I said enthusiastically. "They had to pick it up! How dumb would it have been if some had starved because they refused to take what God was providing."

Sam sounded thoughtful. "I'd be a lot more hungry right now if we hadn't asked those guys for their leftover pizza."

"Right," I said, nodding. "We prayed for God's provision, right? We prayed that He would bless us and give us what we need. But then when it walked by, we had to make our move. Asking and receiving means different things out here on the streets than back home. But the idea is the same."

Sam didn't look nearly impressed enough by my line of logic. So I kept at it.

"Just like you said," I continued, "we'd be a lot more hungry if we hadn't asked for that pizza. God answered our prayers for provision, but we still had to ask these guys for it. We still had to 'pick up the manna.'"

Now Sam was nodding. "I wonder how much we miss because we're unwilling to pick it up. That verse in Matthew, 'Knock and the door will be opened,' why have the door opened if you don't walk through?"

"I know," I said. "Kinda scary."

"It's like asking God to bless your day, then when He puts a needy, smelly person in front of you that you could really help, you wonder what you did to deserve such rotten luck."

"Yep!" I agreed.

We both felt insightful, mature, brilliant to the point of genius. Manna does that to you.

In no time at all, we were back to strumming and yelling.

BLOODY SANDALS

The sore on my foot seemed to be getting worse. It had been there for nearly two weeks, ever since we arrived in San Francisco and I had tripped, pulling the tongue of my right flip-flop out of the sole. Now, to keep the thinning sandal from falling off, I had to walk with my foot out to the side.

But that was awkward and had caused the leather strap to rub continuously, which had led to a blister, which had then festered.

One Saturday afternoon in Berkeley I carelessly scraped the side of my foot against a curb. I winced.

"Does that thing hurt?" Sam asked, pointing to the injury that was now dripping blood.

"Oh, not so much anymore—until just now, that is," I said. "Maybe I'm getting used to it."

"It looks infected to me," said Sam. "You don't want your foot to fall off."

"Sure don't!" I said. "Maybe I should try to fix my flip-flop before we go on."

"Me, too," Sam said, grabbing his own sandal. He'd broken his just days after my accident. We had both tried different repair strategies. Our best idea relied on duct tape—lots of it— but our supply was dwindling. Anyway, the duct tape solution only lasted a day or two. I had even tried several times to walk barefoot but had quit when street people kept warning me to watch out for needles.

"I've got an idea," Sam said. He reached into his pack and pulled out some dental floss we'd gotten at the rescue mission in Portland. "Do you still have that sewing kit?"

I pulled out a $1.99 sewing kit I'd picked up somewhere in Portland to try and patch my jeans and handed it to Sam, who quickly threaded a needle with dental floss. Then he shoved the tongue of his sandal through the hole in its sole and tried to push the needle through the dense plastic. The needle broke with a loud snap. "Watch out for needles," I said. We both burst out laughing.

"You got another one?" asked Sam.

137

"Yep!" I said, handing him one of my two remaining needles. Sam tried again, and this time succeeded. Then we turned to my flip-flop. Before long, we'd tied off the dental floss, put on our new shoes, and grabbed our packs.

We headed uphill past a long stretch of the University of California campus. Our destination: a subway grate that had been recommended by another homeless guy. Although it was rumored to be a popular spot, the grate was vacant when we arrived. So we rolled out our bags and stretched out for the night, tired but thankful for a place to rest.

The grate was warm, but it was also loud. Somewhere deep below us huge fans throbbed relentlessly, pumping exhaust-laden air from deep in the BART system tunnels. Sam and I had to yell to be heard over the roar of the fans. Still, we each fell asleep quickly. If you're tired enough you don't let a little roar here and there keep you awake.

But when we woke up the next morning, we were miserable. Our ears were ringing, our eyes burned and watered, our noses hurt, and our mouths were parched.

"This can't be good," I croaked, feeling my way off of the grate onto some nearby grass. Sam followed. We lay there face down for a while, coughing.

"I guess that wasn't a great place to sleep," I said. "No wonder nobody was on it when we arrived!"

"No kidding! That exhaust almost killed us!"

We waited until our eyes and lungs cleared up, then, since it was Sunday, grabbed our packs and set off toward a large church we had heard about.

When we arrived, we discovered we'd missed the starting time by half an hour. Then we noticed another, smaller church nearby whose sign announced that a service was just about to start.

Between my hurting foot and my aching lungs, I must have begun to worry. We were walking up the sidewalk toward the church when I asked, "Do you think there'll be any long-term effects of this trip?"

"Don't know," replied Sam. "Probably. You can't eat out of the trash and breathe exhaust all night and expect to stay healthy."

"Then again, I guess we aren't supposed to expect circumstances to be easy or safe just because we've prayed about them. We're supposed to go into them knowing that we'll be given what we need, when we need it."

"Amen, bro," Sam said.

Just then I tripped on an uneven piece of sidewalk and smashed my right big toe into the cement, splitting it open and breaking my newly repaired flip-flop. When I stumbled forward under the weight of my pack, I tripped again on the broken flip-flop.

Despite the intense pain, I joined Sam in a good laugh and limped the rest of the way up to the church, my broken flip-flop getting slippery with blood.

Conversations at the front door stopped as we walked up. I had to ask for a church bulletin from the girl who was handing them out. She looked at us as if we had just escaped from a wildlife preserve. But we headed inside for the service anyway and found an empty pew three from the front. The whole room couldn't hold more than a hundred, so our chances of going unnoticed were not good.

We still had a few minutes before the service began, and

139

Sam had an idea. "I'm going to ask the pastor if he can help us out with some food. My stomach is growling." He got up and walked away, but was back shortly, looking disgusted.

"You wouldn't believe what just happened," he said. "So, I went and asked for the pastor. He was standing in the back, getting some coffee. I asked him if he could help us out, if he could hook us up with someone who could feed us. I told him we didn't have any money, that the panhandling here was bad."

Sam paused and shook his head. "You know what he said? He said, 'That's not what we do here. We're here to worship. We can't confuse our purpose.'"

"Wow…," I said, slowly.

"I didn't have anything to say to that, so I just nodded and walked away," Sam said.

"Well, I understand his point," I said, thinking. "This isn't a rescue mission or a soup kitchen. But I *was* hungry. Now I'm frustrated and hungry!"

The theme of the sermon was memorable: "Women shall be saved through childbearing."

In Berkeley, California.

In the year 2003.

At the benediction, the pastor spread his arms wide and with a shiny smile loudly proclaimed, "May the Lord bless you and keep you! May He turn His face to you and give you peace!" I felt like I was going to be sick.

While people filed out, Sam and I kept our seats, journaling and trying to capture the moment and our frustrations.

After a few minutes, three guys came through the pews to talk.

"Hey guys, I'm Drew," one guy said, extending his hand. We introduced ourselves and told them we were living on the streets. After that, the talk rambled around general topics. When I could see the conversation was going nowhere, I decided to try an experiment. (I'll admit my reaction was a little harsh, and done out of frustration, but still…)

I set my backpack on the pew between us. Then I reached down and grabbed my broken flip-flop, and set it atop the pack. Some of the blood was still wet, but most of it had dried, caking the sandal in a dull brown.

"Man, look at all that blood," I said, looking to Sam and pointing to my sandal.

"Bro, does that hurt?" Sam asked, catching onto my experiment.

"A little," I said, reaching for my bag. "It's because my flip-flop is broken. You see?" I said, looking up at the guys and pulling on the broken tongue of the flip-flop.

They nodded but said nothing. I pulled out the dwindling roll of duct tape and ripped off a long piece—a really long piece, stretching it loudly across in front of me the full length of my arms.

"It's such a bummer to walk around all day with broken shoes," I said, shaking my head. "Bad blisters. Bad blisters."

For the next two minutes I proceeded to work intently on fixing my flip-flop while the men watched. Nobody said anything. Occasionally I would interject a comment about how lame my shoes were, how badly my foot hurt, wondering aloud if I might have to get it cut off if the gangrene got bad enough. When I finished, I dropped the sandal and slipped my foot into it.

"Well done!" Sam said.

Drew agreed. "Quite a process!" he said.

"Yep," I agreed and waited.

"Well," Drew said, looking around, "We've got to take off, but it was a pleasure talking with you." He squeezed my shoulder as he left. "I'm praying for you," he said. "You too," he said to Sam.

And the three walked away.

Shocked, Sam and I carried our packs and guitars out into a bright, sunny Berkeley day. As we walked toward People's Park, I broke our silence with a question.

"Why do we so often overlook obvious ways to show the love of God we so loudly proclaim?" Without waiting for an answer, I charged on. "If someone's thirsty, give them a drink! If someone's hungry, feed them! I mean, this is not complicated stuff."

Sam agreed. "Who is to show the world Christ's love if not the church?"

"No one," I said definitively. Then I stopped and looked directly at Sam, who had also stopped. "Do you feel loved?"

"Nope."

"Do you feel fed?"

"Nope. I'm starving! What about you?"

"I'm starving and my feet hurt, and that guy back there knows it. But, hey, he's praying for us."

BERKELEY BOOK YAH

By now the wear and tear of our weeks on the streets had given Sam and me something like the fearsome look of Old Testament prophets. You know—rugged, weather-worn, shaggy, and a little scary. The strange part was that we were beginning to feel the part, too. Across this land we strode (okay, hobbled), looking for a "remnant of God's faithful people," those still passionate in both word and deed to honor Him. It seemed as though there weren't any left, and those out-of-touch but oh-so-religious folks we'd just met in church confirmed our doubts.

Sam and I had just walked into People's Park. We saw a man on the ground, crumpled in a heap where he had fallen, whiskey bottle still clutched in his hand. Hippies danced naked around a tree while onlookers mocked. Where was God in all this? More to the point, where were His people?

Then we met Russ.

Earlier, someone had told us we'd find a group holding a church service Sunday afternoons in the park. Rumors of sack lunches also helped to draw us on till we found them.

It was a group of about twenty. Some wore khaki shorts and button-down shirts while others were obviously street people. Two guitarists were leading worship. As Sam and I set our packs down, several in the crowd nodded a welcome.

143

A Christian homeless guy next to us said enthusiastically, "This is where church should be! It's where the gospel meets the world, because this is where *we* are!" He motioned around the park, pointing to a drug deal taking place, and to the drunk still passed out on the ground. "Jesus came for us, too," he said. "It's a shame when churches kick us out."

The group leader followed with a clear, simple message while other park people wandered in. When he was done, one of the guitarists started clapping. "Do you know how old the speaker is?" he asked all of us in the circle. "He's seventeen years old! A true man after Jesus!" Wow, Sam and I were impressed!

Then the church folks opened two large coolers and handed out lunch. The sandwiches were huge and *fresh*—a rarity on the streets. While everybody ate and visited, the guitarist who had applauded the speaker came over. His name was Russ, and he wanted to know if Sam and I were getting enough to eat. Then, without waiting for a response, he grabbed two more sack lunches and handed them to us. "You guys look like you can eat a *lot!*" he said.

Tattoos covered Russ' arms, suggesting a previous and different lifestyle, but freshly drawn across both wrists, two words stood out boldly: "JESUS CHRIST."

Russ opened an extra large bag of potato chips to share, and while we munched and worked on our sandwiches, he asked questions. He wanted to know where we were headed. We told him Phoenix.

"Excellent! Phoenix is nice and hot!" Russ said with a smile. "How are you going to get there?"

"Well," I said, "we're kind of wondering that ourselves. We usually just cruise into a city, play the guitar and panhandle, and save up enough to move on."

Sam broke in. "But panhandling in San Francisco sucks! We've hardly made any money—hardly enough to live on, and definitely not enough to get bus tickets out of here."

Russ wanted to know more. We described our routines in San Francisco—panhandling in the Haight, hanging out near Golden Gate Park, sleeping by St Mary's. "There's a sweet church that does lunch weekdays," Sam said. "Then Saturdays and Sundays we scrounge. We eat a lot of ninety-nine-cent hamburgers from McDonalds, too."

"So you guys only eat one meal a day?" Russ asked.

We said yes—unless you count a ninety-nine-cent hamburger as a meal, then we ate two.

"Sounds rough," Russ said. He looked like he was contemplating what to do next. Then he stood, said he'd be right back, and left. Sam and I kept eating. A few minutes later, he was back, looking excited. With him was the teenage preacher.

"Guys, this is James," said Russ.

"Great sermon today, James," I said, extending a hand.

"Thanks, but all glory to God," said James, pointing up.

"Check this out," Russ said, so excited he could hardly contain himself. "James and I were talking about it and we want to help you guys out. We want you to come to our church later tonight and stick around for the evening service. Then you can come over to our place to hang out, shower, and get some grub. There are some awesome sisters who can cook a mean meal and they want to help you, too. Then, we'll see if we can get together enough cash for you to get to Phoenix."

Sam and I had both stopped chewing and were staring back and forth between Russ and James.

"Are you serious?" I asked, astounded.

Russ nodded.

"Why?" I asked again.

"Are you in need?" James asked.

"Yeah, I guess we're in a tight spot," I said.

"The Bible says that we must reach out to those in need," James replied. "Jesus loves us, so we get to love you. It's a privilege."

If months on the streets hadn't hardened my emotions, I probably would have starting weeping. We looked wretched and smelled worse. I had that disgusting problem with my foot. And these men had no idea we, too, were Christians. Yet they were offering in the name of Christ to befriend us and meet our needs.

"It really frustrates me when Christians talk about their

faith in Christ but never let the fruit of it grow in their lives," James said quietly. "True faith is visible."

"Yeah, us too, believe me!" I said. "But be encouraged. You two are the first Christians in all our time on the streets who have offered so much help, no questions asked."

James and Russ looked surprised.

"No one?" James asked.

"No one," said Sam. "Thanks for living your faith. It is powerful."

"Well," said James, "if we don't, something's wrong. Jesus said, 'By your love for one another they will know you are my disciples.'"

We visited some more, and before they left, Russ and James again invited us to join them for the evening. "It would be rad if you came," Russ said.

Sam and I spent the rest of the afternoon relaxing in the park. Then, as a bank of fog approached across the bay and the air began to cool, we set off for the mile and a half walk to the church.

In the foyer, we met with our first surprise. We were greeted warmly. Then we were shown where we could stash our guitars and packs and walked to an empty pew. Then two guys actually sat down with us.

While the four of us were talking, Russ ran up. "My boys!" he said breathlessly. "How ya doin'?" He hugged both of us across the pew. "This is great!" he exclaimed. "I was praying you guys would come. Do you have a minute? I want to show you something. Follow me."

Russ led us out to the parking lot to an older white car and popped the trunk.

"This is all for you guys," he said. Inside was a grocery bag full of granola bars, bananas, canned beans, cookies, and peanut butter. Russ beamed as Sam and I stared speechless. "Oh, and this, too," he said, pulling out an envelope stuffed with cash out of his back pocket. "James checked on-line. This should be enough to get you to Phoenix."

With that he stuffed the envelope into my hand and gave us a big hug. "I love you guys, really," Russ said. "And none of that fake crap—I mean it."

The rest of the evening was filled with acts of love (none of that fake crap): an awesome church service; a beautifully prepared meal; a long, hot shower; good conversation; supplies for the road. Russ and James even made sure we found new flip-flops.

The words "Jesus loves you" take on a whole different meaning when you're down and out. You hear them differently. You need them more. Just saying them to the next desperate person you meet could change his day. Wrap those words in friendship, a home-cooked meal, bus fare, and you could change his life.

PHOENIX

"We do not want anger and joy to neutralize each other and produce a surely contentment. We want a fiercer delight and a fiercer discontent."

G. K. CHESTERTON, ORTHODOXY

Start: September 28th, 2003
End: October 17th, 2003
Duration: 19 days
Location: Downtown Phoenix, Main Public Library, other parts of town, Tempe

Carrying a heavy pack for long distances in one-hundred-degree heat just doesn't make sense. Unfortunately, Phoenix gave Sam and me many opportunities to feel like idiots.

Everything in Phoenix is spread out. We couldn't just walk between a rescue mission and a library, or a good pan-handling area and a good place to spend the night like we had in previous cities. Relationships were harder, too—we only ran into other homeless people we knew every three or four days. We worked for a carnival at the northwest end of town, stayed in the southeast, ate meals in the southwest, and went to church in the northeast. That meant long bus rides, which meant we needed cash for tickets.

Sam and I passed as much time in the city's air-conditioned main library as we could. It didn't open until 10 A.M., though, and the temperature was already climbing into the nineties by then. Not that the locals seemed to notice. On one one-hundred-plus-degree day, a man we met on a bus complained that he was cold (Arizonans, we decided, suffer from heat-induced delusions). The heat and dry air made dehydration a constant concern, and we used gas station restrooms to replenish our water supply whenever the libraries were closed.

Several of the churches that we encountered in Phoenix left us thirsty, too. Of course, the body of Christ in one city doesn't represent every city, and our experience only tells a slice of the story. But we experienced big programs, big churches, and big talk, without much love in action, at least for two unappealing transients like us.

To be fair, Sam and I were running out of patience and strength. Phoenix marked a turning point: We felt we had met the challenge of the streets and survived; now we just wanted it all to end. The months of stress and hardship, and now the furnace of Phoenix heat, had worn us down. Eight days earlier than planned, we left for San Diego.

WE DON'T GO TO CHURCH

Although Sam and I had spent every Sunday morning at a church somewhere on our travels, the lack of community was taking a toll on us. Even at church, we felt isolated because of how we looked, how we smelled, and who people perceived us to be. In fact, walking into a church where we hoped to find genuine fellowship only to be met by condescension or suspicion or disingenuous flattery was the worst kind of rejection.

One night in Phoenix we stretched out our sleeping bags in front of a church's main doors hoping that early the next morning we would be awakened by a kindhearted churchgoer wondering if he could help us in some way. A simple, obvious plan, we thought, but it didn't work.

At about seven the next morning, while a dream of wintertime in the Rockies cooled my sweating body, a far away voice pulled me back to reality. "And before we read from Romans 8, let us pray together..."

Sam and I were still on the steps of the church and already baking in the morning sun. I rolled over to look through the sanctuary windows. A small gathering was standing while the pastor led in prayer. The early service was just getting under way inside, but for us, the voice came from a speaker just above where we slept.

151

"Sam," I said, nudging him awake.

"Yeah?" He sat up, shaking his head.

"Did anybody wake you up?" I said, pointing into the sanctuary.

"No way," he said. We both realized what had happened. Every person inside had gone through a side door. "Nobody woke me up. You?"

"Nope."

The pastor was ending his prayer. "Lord, teach us to look not unto ourselves but unto You and unto others..." With a loud amen that came metallically through the speaker above, the congregation took its seat and he began his sermon.

Already soaked with sweat, we decided to pack up and

move on. "Wow," said Sam, "I thought we were making it easy for them!"

But were we? I'm not so sure now. I think two sleeping transients on the church steps early one morning would make most people uneasy, Christian or not. The need is unexpected, out of place, and a little disturbing. Yet it is exactly here, in the difficult circumstances, that Christ's love should take risks to meet needs. In *A Ragamuffin Gospel,* Brennan Manning describes what that kind of love looks like: "To evangelize a person is to say to him or her: you too are loved by God and the Lord Jesus. And not only to say it but to really think it, and relate it to them so they can sense it. But that becomes possible only by offering the person your friendship, a friendship that is real, unselfish, without condescension, full of confidence and profound esteem."

152

- - -

One church we visited took up nearly the whole side of a mountain, with buildings spread over acres of beautifully landscaped and irrigated grounds. We walked past large fountains spraying cool water as we entered the main sanctuary. The place sat thousands, and it was packed. A dozen TV cameras were pointed at the stage or roamed the aisles.

The pastor opened the service up by explaining that the ensuing worship concert and teaching service would be recorded for a DVD that would be distributed around the world.

Sam and I sat there feeling extremely out of place. Being ripped in a moment from our sidewalk existence of nothing to do, nothing to eat, and nowhere to be and dropped into a multi-million-dollar worship "production" was too much of a shock.

The program got under way. Everything—talent, facilities, production—was first-rate. Cameras rolled continuously and the lighting rotated through a hundred hues while the fog machines pumped a white haze across the vast stage. The two lead singers wore flashy designer clothing that I was sure cost more than Sam and I had lived on for the past four months.

After a while, I rose to use the restroom. I did have to go, but really I needed to escape the thundering confusion in my head.

Fortunately, the men's room was first-rate, too. I set to scrubbing my hands and face to the booming bass line coming through the walls from the concert. When I scrubbed, the water in the clean white sink turned a dull gray.

Then two large men walked in. They were dressed in black suits and wore security-police earpieces. To my surprise, it quickly became apparent that they were there to see me.

Noticing in the mirror that neither was smiling, I turned off the water and turned around to face them.

"Gentlemen," I said with a nod.

"Sir, did you just attempt to run on stage?" the man on the left asked.

The question seemed so weighted I had to ask him to repeat himself just to keep from laughing. "Sir, did you just attempt to run on stage and disrupt the service?" The man sounded somewhat agitated.

"No, sir, I did not. I've been in here for the last three minutes, and before that I was at my seat in the sanctuary."

"Are you sure?" the other man asked.

"Yes, I'm *sure!* I've been standing right here trying to clean up," I replied. Then I decided to go deep. "Did *you* see me run on stage?"

153

"Okay then," the first man said, ducking my question. "Why don't you finish, uh, cleaning up here then come speak to us outside."

"Okay," I said, grabbing a few paper towels and turning back to face the mirror. After drying myself off, I wiped down the sink.

Only one of the men was waiting for me when I emerged, but he walked right over to me.

"Sir, I'm going to ask you one more time. Did you try to get up on stage?"

I told him again that I hadn't. What was driving his question, I asked.

"Someone tried to get on stage, and the only witness said that the man had dread locks," he replied. "You have dread locks."

"That's true, but I didn't try to get on stage."

The man thought for a moment, then said, "Okay, I believe you. Are you going back to your seat now?"

"Yes…" I said, feeling suddenly tentative.

"I'll escort you back," the man said, falling in step behind me. When I took my seat, the security guard remained by the door through which I had entered so he could keep an eye on me.

Sam nodded toward the security guard with a questioning look in my direction. I shook my head and told him I would explain later. For the rest of the service, I personally felt very safe, and I observed no other criminal activity whatsoever. Everything went smoothly—cameras, lights, singers, preacher, security guards, fog machine.

It was the perfect church program. And now it's available all over the world on DVD.

- - -

There is a church in my hometown that refuses to have anything to do with the other churches around. Whenever other pastors or lay persons in the community have tried to bridge the gap, the church holds up its long and divisive list of mandatory beliefs. Since no one else quite agrees with the entire list, no fellowship is permitted. The result? Disunity and division among believers, and muted laughter from everyone else. The body of Christ in my town, I'd have to say, walks with a bad limp.

Last summer a large, popular Christian music group held a worship concert at a large arena in Denver. Along with a number of my friends from church, I attended. It was an awesome sight—fifteen thousand people united in worship, hands raised together to honor the Lord. About halfway through the evening, I noticed twenty or so members were there from the church in my hometown that refused to have anything to do with other churches. There they were, lifting their hands alongside members of the same family, in worship to the same God. We were finally united.

An arena event can do that, I guess. It's wonderful that we were joined together in worship. But it's sad that our unity only lasted for an hour and cost $37.50.

We don't *go* to church, we *are* the church. So many problems that show up on the church steps, or in the pews, or between congregations seem to start with misunderstandings about that. The church isn't a physical building or a doctrinal statement or a perfectly produced program. It is us—we are the living expression of Christ's presence in the world, His

155

body. The sooner we realize that, the sooner we'll be able to be the healing body of Christ to our sin-sick world.

RETURN TO FORGIVENESS

I awoke, rolled over, and saw beads of sweat already forming on my arms. Saturday, early morning, Phoenix.

I reached for my glasses, shoved them onto my face, and watched as the world snapped into focus. During our trip I couldn't have afforded to spend food money on saline solution for contacts. Glasses were the only option if I wanted to see anything.

Sam and I had spent the night on an out-of-the-way piece of lawn that was part of a large church campus. Early as it was, carloads of people were already pulling up to a door on a building not far away. We saw what looked like stainless steel buffet containers being carried indoors. Vivid pictures of omelets, donuts, fruit, and coffee instantly came to mind.

"You awake?" Sam asked, also eyeing the activity.

"Yep," I replied. "Wonder what's going on over there. Think they have a Saturday morning service?"

"I don't know. Maybe."

Sam and I both reached into our backpacks and grabbed our Bibles and journals. Mind you, it wasn't to make some kind of statement—these quiet times had become our normal morning habit on the streets.

About ten minutes later two men walked up. They were nicely dressed and moved with an air of authority, especially the guy in the white polo shirt.

"How's it going, guys?" I said as they approached.

"You need to leave," the man in the white shirt said blankly.

"Oh, really? Why?" Sam asked, obviously taken aback by the guy's frankness. Didn't they see we were reading our Bibles?

"You heard me. You need to leave," he said again. "You can't sit outside the sanctuary like this. We've got a lot of people coming today, and you can't be here." Without waiting for a response, he turned and both men continued marching into the sanctuary.

"Huh," I said, perplexed. "Didn't expect *that*."

I guess Sam was feeling as cantankerous as I, because we both quickly decided we weren't quite ready to leave. "Let's hold on a while and see what happens," I said, and we turned back to our reading and journaling.

We didn't have to wait long. In five minutes, both men were back, and the man in the white polo shirt was fuming.

"What's the deal, guys? I told you you need to leave and you haven't moved!"

157

"Yes, sir, I realize that," I said, trying to be as polite as possible. "But we don't understand why."

"I told you why!" The man's face reddened. Slowly, struggling to control his tone and volume, he restated his reason. "We've got...something going on...and you're not supposed to be on...church grounds!"

I'll admit, I gave up on polite at that point. Throwing my journal at my backpack, I said, "Sir, forgive me for being troublesome, but *what* are church grounds for?"

"This is nonsense!" the man yelled. By now, he looked like he was going to blow a gasket. "We could stand here all day debating what church grounds are for! The fact is, they're not for this and you need to leave—now!"

With that he turned, and both men stormed away again.

After a moment or two of silence, Sam had a profound reaction. "Wow," he said.

My next thought was profound, too. "Del Taco burritos are only forty-nine cents," I said. "And it's about a mile away."

Neither of us wanted to think through how disgusted we felt. If there is any place on this earth, any group of people in which a person *must* sense welcome acceptance of their presence, it is the church.

"Yeah," Sam agreed. "I need to use the bathroom, too, and brush my teeth."

We packed and started walking.

A mile-long walk carrying packs on a hot Phoenix morning is a very long mile. We were sweating and miserable in no time. But as we walked, we prayed.

They were honest, complaining, frustrated prayers. They were prayers, too, asking for forgiveness for our attitudes. And they were prayers for the man in the white polo shirt—for his conviction, and for the church he protected so annoyingly well from people like us.

- - -

The next morning we were back at the same Del Taco, cleaning up as best we could in the bathroom. It was Sunday, and we had a church we intended to visit.

Guess which one.

After a scrub and a bite of breakfast, we retraced our steps from the day before. Again, it was a scorching mile, and by the time we walked into the church lobby, we were dripping and radiating the stench of life in the open.

"Welcome to our church," an usher said, forcing a smile.

"Good to be here!" we replied. But we meant it.

In the cool sanctuary, we found an open pew, took our packs off, and sat down, uncomfortably conscious of the murmurs and stares.

The lights dimmed and the service began—a choir, followed by a more contemporary band. Toward the end of the music service, I looked around. The church was packed—except for three rows ahead of us and three behind, as well as the full length of our pew. In that empty circle, there wasn't another worshiper to be found.

The pastor's sermon, which lasted precisely thirty-five minutes, was interjected with occasional enthusiastic amens from around the sanctuary. I leaned over to Sam.

"What says more about who you are in Christ—how loudly you say *amen!* in the service or how well you treat strangers in the foyer?" We were both still feeling testy.

Then a most surprising thing happened. After the benediction, as Sam and I prepared to leave, we heard a familiar voice.

"Guys! Guys!" It was Mr. White Polo Shirt, and he was rushing toward us.

I let my pack drop, which was a good thing, because when he reached us, he threw his arms around us both in a tight embrace. When he let go, we saw tears streaming down his face.

"Guys, I'm so sorry," he began. "And I'm so glad you came back. Forgive me for what I said and did yesterday. Forgive me…" His voice trailed off. "I can't believe I did that. We were having a church breakfast. I kicked you out of the church when I should have invited you in. Really, I'm sorry. By the way, I'm Terry."

Of course, Sam and I were in shock. We had prayed for this man, but, well, never expected *this*.

"That's okay, man," I said. I put my hand on his shoulder. "Honestly it's okay. We forgive you. See, we've been traveling for a while, met some church folk...and we're almost used to it by now."

"But that's just it," said Terry. "You *shouldn't* be used to it. Christians should never make you accustomed to rejection. If there is anywhere you should be accepted and loved, it should be at a church."

We all began to relax. Terry explained how he'd been convicted the previous day as soon as we'd left. He had actually jumped in his car and gone looking for us, hoping he could bring us back to join in the breakfast.

And then he shared the most surprising fact of all. He said, "I'm the director of a homeless outreach program in the area. I should know better."

He looked back and forth between us for a second, crestfallen—then all three of us burst out laughing. We all agreed we were extremely thankful that love covers a multitude of wrongs.

As we parted on the front steps of the church, we thanked Terry again for his honesty and humility. "You made our day," I told him. "Heck, you've made our whole month!"

You can never tell what the Spirit is up to in a heart, whether it's beating under a crisp, white polo shirt or a filthy, torn, brown one. You never know what God is up to inside His people everywhere, or inside the buildings they dedicate to Him.

I wonder what would have happened if Sam and I had decided not to return to that church Sunday morning. Love can't cover wrongs if we let frustrations and failures keep us apart.

FIX OR FISH SANDWICH?

We decided to try Tempe. Maybe the college atmosphere with students on every street would make the panhandling easier than in downtown Phoenix. Or maybe it wouldn't. After all, most students don't have extra cash lying around.

With our last couple of dollars Sam and I bought bus tickets. The trip took about an hour, but that was fine by us—the bus was air-conditioned and not very crowded, so we stretched out, enjoying the cool luxury. In Tempe, though, it seemed as though the thermostat had been cranked up even higher than downtown. We walked about a mile in the wrong direction but finally backtracked and found a large bookstore where we spent the rest of the day in order to escape the heat.

When the bookstore closed at six, Sam and I didn't have much else to do but head out onto the cement to earn money for dinner. The streets were crowded, everyone enjoying the relative coolness of the evening. Sam and I set up on a promising stretch of sidewalk and played our hearts out.

After only a couple of hours we had made nearly thirty dollars—more than enough for us to buy dinner at a nearby sandwich shop and, when we were ready, bus tickets back downtown. We decided to eat and find a place for the night.

By this time in the trip, Sam and I had developed pretty good instincts for places we would feel comfortable spending the night. When we had gotten off the bus earlier in the day, we'd noticed a group of trees next to a small white church. We'd both made a mental note that it might make for a good night's sleep, and now we headed back in that direction.

As Sam and I walked toward our spot for the night, we passed a panhandler who clearly didn't share in our earlier success. He was aggressive—often demanding—and insulting. People were doing everything they could to avoid or ignore him.

"What do you two want?" the man snarled as Sam and I looped back to talk to him.

"Just want to see if we can help out," I said as pedestrians flowed around us. "I'm Mike."

"Karl." Then, by way of answering me, he yelled at a nicely-dressed couple approaching, "If you could help these people understand that I'M STARVING, that'd be great!" The couple veered quickly away.

"Hey, man," Sam said, trying to calm him down. "We'll get you some food if you want. You don't need to scream at people."

"Really?" Karl did not appear interested in Sam's offer. "Hey, 'scuse me, ma'am? Ma'am!" he yelled at the next passerby. "Could you spare some change for some dinner?"

Sam persisted. "Hey, Karl," he said, touching the guy's shoulder to get his attention, "we'll buy you dinner. See, there's a McDonald's right there. What do you want?"

"Fish sandwich," Karl said, then pushed both of us out of the way in order to catch up to another couple to beg.

"I'll go," Sam said to me, slinging off his pack and setting it against the building.

"Get him a whole meal," I said.

"Definitely," Sam said, and he ran across the street to McDonald's.

Karl didn't settle down to wait for dinner. Not for a second. In fact, he seemed to get pushier and more obnoxious with every passing minute. "I need some *food!*" he screamed at a woman who scurried past.

I began to get frustrated. This man was ruining a lot of people's evening for no reason.

"Karl!" I said sharply enough to catch his attention and stop him in mid sentence.

"Yeah?" he said, startled.

"What are you doing? Sam and I are buying you a fish sandwich *meal.* Sandwich, fries, and a drink! Sam will be right back with it."

Karl came close, shoved his face into mine and squinted at me. "You think that's what I really want? I already ate dinner. I need a fix, man. I need a fix."

The gritty reality of Karl's situation slammed home, and I felt foolish. Sam and I had been taken in. We should have been better by now at telling the difference between the need for food and the craving for drugs. Hunger makes a person listless and compliant. A need for a fix makes a person desperate and obnoxious.

I didn't really know whether I should stop Sam as he walked up to Karl carrying the heavy golden arches bag. So I decided to watch and see what happened.

"Here you go, bro," Sam said, offering the super-sized drink and large bag of food to Karl.

"Put it against the wall, would ya?" said Karl.

"I thought you said you were hungry, bro!" Sam said, confused.

"Yeah, yeah, I am." But Karl wasn't even looking at Sam. "Sir, spare a quarter?" he said. "Hey, you there! I need some change!"

163

I looked at Sam. "Don't worry about it. Let's just leave the food. He'll eat it if he wants to."

"Enjoy, Karl," Sam said setting the bag and drink down. We gathered our packs to leave. But Karl didn't miss a beat. "I'M STARVING, LADY! Can't you *see* that?" we heard him yelling as we walked away.

"What was that all about?" Sam asked once we were out of earshot.

"He's in it for the drugs, not for the food," I said with a sigh. "We sure read him wrong." Addiction can cheat you every time, even if you're just the person who's trying to help.

We walked toward the trees and the small white church, feeling frustrated, hoping that our instincts for picking a place to sleep hadn't let us down, too.

ON BEGGING

"Anything to make a buck" as the saying goes, and homeless people are no exception. We saw some pretty interesting methods used for eliciting a donation. The most hilarious belonged to the "Bush Man" in San Francisco. He would cut some branches from a nearby park tree and stand in the middle of a sidewalk holding it, hidden from view. Then, when an unsuspecting pedestrian walked past, he would leap out and scare the person. Money came streaming into his collection bucket, not from his startled victims, but from the crowd who gathered on the other side of the street to watch the fright fest and erupt into laughter with every new encounter.

One evening in Phoenix, as Sam and I played outside a restaurant, a group of other homeless guys walked past, one of them wearing a cardboard sign that said, "Ignore me for $1.00."

Directly in front of us where we were sitting, a group of girls read the sign and burst out laughing, commenting on the guy's originality. One reached into her purse and handed him a dollar. But as he turned around to thank her, he noticed Sam and me, empty guitar cases open, playing nearby. He immediately walked over and put the dollar into our case. "Sorry, man," he said, "I didn't see you guys working here." (We saw this kind of territorial respect often on the streets.)

"No problem! Thanks a lot!" we said. But the girls all turned away when I looked back in their direction. They were avoiding the awkward situation of admitting they had ignored us, ironically, by ignoring us.

We actually did fairly well that night. Playing where people can walk quickly past usually resulted in a lot of pretending that we didn't exist. But, when people had to stand in lines, as seemed to be the case outside restaurants, and when they *couldn't* walk away, it was more difficult to ignore us.

But that raises an important question: *Should* you give money to the beggars? You run into them in every major American city—standing at the off-ramp on your way home from work, sitting at busy intersections on your lunch break, or walking up to you when you're downtown for an evening with friends.

The simple answer is, "probably not," but I need to qualify that.

Obviously, Sam and I survived on just such donations. And we met other homeless men and women whose only income was from money dropped into a hat or cup.

Unfortunately, it's also true that a significant portion of the men and women we knew on the streets would—within a half hour of receiving a donation—spend it entirely on drugs

165

or alcohol. A nugget of marijuana or crack is only five dollars, and a forty-ounce beer is only two-fifty. So your money is probably providing someone with their fix before you even get home or back to the office.

That's why I recommend you give something other than cash. For example, gift certificates to fast-food restaurants make a good alternative. They're easy, quick, and helpful, and you know your gift isn't going to support a destructive habit, at least not directly. Popular coffee shops also issue gift certificates, as do many grocery store chains (you can get a coupon that can only be used to purchase food).

Having said that, I think the most meaningful gift might be your genuine attention and caring. It was amazing how much a smile or quick hello did for Sam and me on the streets, partly because such kindnesses were so rare. When someone stopped to talk, even for a minute, the powerful underlying message was, "I notice you, you're a human being, and you're worth my time."

If you can, consider buying a take-out meal from a nearby restaurant and sitting with the person while they eat. You'll hear the most incredible stories. While you visit, listen for the leading of the Spirit. You'd be surprised how much you can learn in just a few minutes.

There aren't really easy answers to the question of giving to panhandlers. On the one hand, we're called to help those in need. On the other, we're called to be "wise as serpents, innocent as doves." Being both wise *and* innocent might mean taking some risks, getting creative, and forgiving yourself if you feel foolish or make mistakes.

Whatever response you choose, if you're open to being

used of God and you ask Him for guidance, He *will* show you how to respond in each instance in a way that honors Him and helps to meet real human needs, both seen and unseen.

NIKKI

If life on the streets is tough for men, in many ways it's even more difficult for women.

One evening, as Sam and I were panhandling on a busy street corner, trying to get enough money to buy something to eat, a girl in her late teens came and sat down next to us. She looked as though she had been on the streets of Phoenix for a while: dark tan, filthy skin, matted hair, and ill-fitting, dirty clothes.

We stopped playing our guitars to welcome her.

"How's it going?" Sam asked her with a smile.

"Oh, all right, I suppose." Then, with a laugh that made her cough, she said, "Can't complain when it ain't rainin'!"

"Guess Phoenix has something to offer!" I said with a laugh, extending my hand. "I'm Mike."

"Nikki," she said, shaking my hand and then Sam's.

"Hey, you guys don't have a cigarette I could bum off you, do ya?" Nikki asked, looking hopeful.

We shook our heads. "No, sorry."

She looked down at our guitar case, where our seed money had grown into a few dollars.

"Mind if I bum a quarter so I can get one before I go to sleep?"

"No, I guess not," I said, looking at Sam to be sure he was okay with it.

He shrugged. "Sure, go ahead."

"How long have you been in Phoenix, Nikki?" I asked, trying to make conversation.

"My whole life." She had a strange grin on her face. "Born and raised."

"Do you have family here?" Sam asked.

Nikki nodded, but her face turned sour. "But I ain't never goin' back."

"Why not?" Sam and I both asked.

"Because of my jerk of a dad. He beat me one too many times. I ain't never going back. Even street life is better than that life."

We fell silent for a few minutes, dumbfounded by what she had said. What could we say? It must have been pretty awful if Nikki preferred street life to home life.

Nikki broke the silence. "So are you going to play another song?"

Sam and I nodded to one another and started messing around with a simple chord progression that didn't require much thought. Our minds were on Nikki and her situation.

"Nikki, do you have someplace safe to stay the night?" Sam asked after a few minutes.

Nikki nodded but then changed her mind and shook her head. "Nah. But don't worry about me. I'll figure something out. I always do." She stood and started walking down the street from where she'd come a few moments earlier. Looking back over her shoulder, she called out to us. "Thanks, you guys. Your music made my night."

We waved good-bye and watched, saddened, as Nikki walked down the road. She reached a stoplight just as it turned red and stood waiting, tapping her foot on the side-walk. As she stood there, a shiny black pickup truck pulled up to the light, right next to her. The driver of the car honked, and she turned to look. We couldn't hear what they were say-ing, but a moment later, Nikki nodded, the car door opened, and she climbed inside. The light turned green, and the truck sped off into the night.

"Uh-oh," Sam said, looking at me.

I nodded. "That's not good at all."

- - -

Sam and I woke slowly the next morning and took turns watching the bags and guitars as the other used the bathroom at the convenience store across the street. Walking back out of the store into the Phoenix heat was like stepping into an oven set to Broil. By eight o'clock we were already sweating.

We journaled for a few minutes, and then something unexpected happened.

There, on the streets a few blocks away, someone was walking toward us with her head hung low. It was Nikki. She was wearing different, cleaner clothes, but she didn't have any shoes. Soon she reached us. Sitting down, she swore under her breath. "Man, that was a bad idea."

"What's that?" I asked.

She pulled her hair back from her face, and Sam and I gasped. Her right cheekbone was swollen and puffy, an hours-old bruise already turning purple.

"Oh no, Nikki. What happened?" Sam asked. But it was obvious.

169

"What do you think happened?" Nikki said through clenched teeth. "He hit me." She looked out into the street as several cars flew past down the road.

We were all silent for a minute, completely at a loss for words.

Anger was boiling up inside me. What kind of a guy hits a homeless teenage girl? "Do you want us to talk to him?"

Nikki shook her head and looked out at the street. "Nah. He's on his way to LA. Besides, I'll never see him again."

"Wait here," Sam said, hopping up and running across the street to the convenience store. He came back a moment later with a cup of ice and a few paper towels Nikki could use on her face. "Here you go. Maybe this ice will help the swelling go down."

"Thanks," she said, taking the ice and paper towels from Sam and pressing several cubes against her swollen face.

"Is there anything we can do for you?" Sam asked with evident concern.

Nikki shook her head again. "No." She swore under her breath, becoming angry. "Gosh, that was a stupid thing to do, wasn't it? I should have known better. A shady guy offers me a meal and a shower, some clean clothes and a place to spend the night, and all of my instincts go flying right out the window."

"Don't be too hard on yourself, Nikki," I said, searching for words. "It's not your fault."

"Yeah," Sam said. "I mean, how long had it been since you'd slept inside?"

Nikki looked back and forth between us, nodding. "A while."

We sat in silence for a few minutes, Sam and me feeling

helpless and Nikki doing the best she could to hide her tears.

Whenever we close our eyes to the real needs of the real people of our world, we force them to survive via whatever options are available to them, dehumanizing though they may be. This means a lot of different things for a lot of different people. For Nikki, the only way she knew to stay off the streets that night was to be with a guy who hit her (and did who knows what else to her) in the first twenty-four hours she knew him.

Nikki stood and started walking down the sidewalk. Before she got too far away, she turned back to us. "Thanks for the ice."

ROAD RASH CARNIVAL

Both Sam and I had lost a significant amount of weight by now. Our clothes were stained and tattered, our bodies reeked, and the grime pressed into the creases and pores of our skin seemed far beyond the reach of soap. Then again, we didn't have any soap, so it wouldn't have mattered anyway.

But it wasn't the accumulating grime of the road life that took us by surprise. It was the mental and emotional grime that seemed to permeate our very beings that we weren't quite prepared for. Of course, it only makes sense that if you hardly ever have a conversation with someone who isn't broken and maimed and defeated by this life that you will start to feel broken and maimed and defeated yourself. Sometimes I felt like there was a different kind of dirt being caked *into* Sam and me. I began to wonder if it could ever be fully washed away.

In Phoenix, time dragged. Twenty-fours had never seemed so endless. We found ourselves becoming more lethargic as the month wore on, more prone to sit listlessly, or to sleep. Emotion, whether tears or laughter, became a luxury. We were simply wearing down. We had road rash. Every activity had some kind of discomfort attached to it, and we could barely summon the will to press on.

How do the men and women who have been enduring the streets for years and even decades manage? By that point in our trip, both Sam and I had a new appreciation for the determination it takes to just keep moving toward the next meal. And despite it all—or maybe because of it—we had a new understanding that God gives you His strength when you need it most.

> *He gives strength to the weary*
> *and increases the power of the weak.*
> *Even youths grow tired and weary,*
> *and young men stumble and fall;*
> *but those who hope in the LORD*
> *will renew their strength.*
> (Isaiah 40:29–31)

One hot afternoon along a boulevard, we were putting one foot in front of the other, trying to get to a southside rescue mission in hopes of finding a shower and a place to sleep. We were both painfully sunburned on almost every exposed skin surface (a piece of newspaper that I'd been using as shade obviously hadn't done the job).

Suddenly a weathered pickup truck careened across three lanes of traffic and came to a screeching halt twenty feet ahead of us. Cars honked furiously as they sped by.

An old man with plenty of hair but few teeth sat in the

front seat staring at us through thick, grease-smudged glasses. Next to him on the seat sat a saggy-eyed basset hound. He stared, too.

The man exhaled a cloud of cigarette smoke. "You boys looking for work?" he asked.

Sam and I looked at each other, each wondering if we were.

Cold, hard cash. Well, it certainly would be nice to have some! The panhandling hadn't been going well. We had started to worry that we'd never be able pull in enough money to buy bus tickets to San Diego.

"How much do you pay?" I asked, wondering if I had it in me to do whatever job this guy was offering in the Phoenix heat.

"Fifty dollars per day," he said. "Each." He winked and exhaled another cloud of smoke.

Sam and I looked at each other, astonished at such a large sum. Sure, at ten hours of work that would be only five dollars per hour, under minimum wage. But still, one day's labor would give us one hundred dollars between the two of us. Neither of us had laid eyes on that much money in five months. It would give us freedom to spend the hottest days in the library downtown instead of trying to panhandle on the hot-as-a-skillet sidewalks of Phoenix. Even better, it would buy us tickets out of town.

"What kind of work?" Sam asked.

"Carnival," the old man said. "I tell you what. Just come straight north on this road until you see two churches on the right-hand side. You'll see the Ferris wheel."

With that the man backed his pickup out into the street, nearly causing another accident. A truck rushing up from behind blasted its horn. The basset hound started baying.

But the man just waved and roared away, leaving Sam and me to decide.

"You realize we could have a hundred dollars by tomorrow evening," I said. The idea almost had me reeling.

"I'm in," said Sam. And that was it.

We limped on to the rescue mission for a meal, then put our last coins together to buy a ride back north on the city bus. There was no missing the carnival. Huge, colorful rides and truck trailers spread out across a large parking lot. But the carnival was moving on. Our job was to tear it down and load the trucks.

We worked for twenty hours straight.

How could something that brings kids so much joy bring two men so much misery? Take the Tilt-a-Whirl. The Tilt-a-Whirl makes kids scream with pleasure while it scrambles their wits and presses their cotton-candy-filled bellies to the red plastic seats. But for the tear down crew, it is simply a vast assembly of fourteen-foot steel structures, each weighing about two hundred pounds. Fortunately, a Tilt-a-Whirl fits nicely onto an eighteen wheeler. Unfortunately, Sam and I—being the "young bucks" according to the older guys on the crew—got the task of heaving these massive steel objects six feet straight up, then sliding them onto the eighteen wheeler.

Dismantling and loading the Tilt-a-Whirl alone took nearly six hours of back-breaking labor that bloodied four of my fingers and blackened one of my toenails. Sam didn't fare any better. We worked through the afternoon and through the night and into the next day with hardly a pause.

When the trucks were finally loaded, Sam and I collapsed in the shade behind the trailer that doubled as the ticket booth. Our foreman had disappeared inside, and we weren't about to leave that ticket-booth-on-wheels until he reemerged with cash. Fifty dollars for each of us.

We laid there comparing bloodied fingers and toes, intermittently groaning or trying to stretch cramping muscles. "You know, Sam," I said, "I've never really wanted to drink or do drugs before. But you know what? After being out here, I can't blame the guys who do stuff like that in order to forget. There's not much out here I want to remember."

When we finally got paid, we knew what to do. We headed straight for the Greyhound bus station.

SAN DIEGO

"Heavenly expectation begins precisely at the moment when earthly expectation sinks down in weakness and despair."

SOREN KIERKEGAARD, EDIFYING DISCOURSES

Start: October 17th, 2003
End: November 2nd, 2003
Duration: 17 days
Location: Downtown, Ocean Beach area

O ur final city. It felt good to be by the ocean again. It was cooler and it made taking a bath easier (although that rarely happened because the water was so cold).

Downtown San Diego proved to be a difficult environment to panhandle or find shelter in. So, after asking around for advice, we headed out to Ocean Beach, a low-key district north and west of downtown.

It seemed like a perfect fit. Other homeless people there greeted us warmly within the first two hours of our arrival. The main street was lined with restaurants and shops we probably couldn't afford, but it ended in a picturesque stretch of beach. Most of our meals would come from a tiny and wonderfully cheap Mexican restaurant on the main strip. We slept near the cliffs with the ocean waves crashing just below.

During our last week, two major wildfires broke out in the hills to the east of the city. The fires turned out to be the worst in San Diego history. Sixteen died in the flames, and more than 2,400 homes burned to the ground.

By then, Sam and I had been on the streets nonstop together for four months. Each day left us feeling more like crossing the finish line.

SHUFFLING HOME

My first introduction to Bob came by way of seeing a teenage boy hanging himself ridiculously out of a truck stopped at a busy intersection, screaming "Hurry up, old man!" at a hunched-over elderly man who was hobbling across the crosswalk.

Bob—I learned later that was his name—hobbled furiously, but not quickly. Inch by excruciating inch, he shuffled his cowboy boots toward his destination—the distant, other side of the street. Even though he never looked up, Bob seemed to know exactly where he was going.

On he shuffled.

Traffic waited. The teenager jeered. I watched, amazed.

Ah, Bob…

That first time I saw him, he was decked out in thick pants, a long-sleeved flannel shirt, and a leather coat—in perfect San Diego weather, mind you. To top things off, he was wearing a beat-up baseball cap with an action figure rubber-banded to the bill.

I met Bob a week or so later. It was a foggy evening in Ocean Beach, and he shuffled right up to me and my guitar case and asked for money to buy coffee from "the ARCO down the street." After a little conversation, I figured the old guy was sincere, so I handed over enough for a large coffee. Bob thanked me with several weak but excited handshakes. That was the beginning of a budding friendship.

Bob seemed to shuffle all over town. Everyone seemed to know him. He'd pause often to speak with another homeless man or woman sitting on a corner or in a doorway. If he didn't stop to speak, his slow nod would evoke a similar nod, or even a "Hey, Bob" as he passed. Bob had been in San Diego for a while.

I used to see Bob making his nightly rounds up and down the street. Slowly, unbelievably slowly he'd pass by, headed toward "the ARCO down the street." Every night he said he needed just a little coffee before retiring. Then he'd head to a nearby parking lot to get his night's sleep in some bushes.

At first I thought that it was his cowboy boots that were slowing him down. They seemed to be stretched way too tightly over his feet. Later, I figured it was his stomach. Whatever the source, pain seemed to go with him at every step.

When Bob talked, he didn't raise his head or his voice, so you had to lean over real close if you wanted to hear. Once, when I tried to buy him a chicken taco from our favorite Mexican restaurant, he declined.

"Oh no," he said softly to the pavement. "No thanks. I can't eat anything like that. My stomach just doesn't work anymore. Anything hard I can't digest."

He mentioned surgeries from earlier in his life that had left him unable to eat anything more complicated than simple peanut butter sandwiches. Well, Sam and I had some peanut butter and a few corn tortillas. So that night, in place of a chicken taco, I offered Bob a tortilla and peanut butter sandwich, which he readily accepted.

Munching happily, he gradually shuffled away.

When I finally asked Bob about his slow gait, he pointed to his worn cowboy boots and stated in a matter-of-fact way that he was going to have several of his toes amputated soon.

"I guess they just sort of rotted," he said. "They called my daughter in Florida, and she's going to come out here and get me after they cut off my toes. She says that I need to come home with her now."

Bob wheezed out a little laugh, but I felt suddenly shattered on his behalf.

"My daughter says I need to sit on a rocking chair and watch the people pass by like a normal old man," he continued. "Guess I'll have to once they cut off my toes."

Several times during our last week in San Diego, Bob mentioned how much he wanted me to meet his daughter when she came to pick him up. But although we tried to connect, it didn't work out.

Late one night during his customary evening walk to "the ARCO down the street" the night prior to his daughter's arrival, Bob stopped to talk for longer than usual. We chatted about the weather and other happenings around town. A few homeless men had left town mysteriously. That worried Bob.

Then he turned and looked straight at me. For the first time, I heard the sound of hope in his voice. "I get to go home, Mike. Real soon. I get to go home."

He patted me on the arm, turned, and shuffled inch by inch away.

I never saw Bob again. He always seemed to know exactly

where he was going, though. I sure hope he made it all the way home.

OLD YELLERS

One cool evening, just a few blocks from the Pacific, I sat pan-handling outside of a liquor store while Sam took a walk. I had discovered that I pulled better tips playing the guitar outside the liquor shop than across the street outside the family restaurant. Drunk people are more generous than sober people.

Occasionally someone would drop a nugget of marijuana in the case, but most people gave change left over from their liquor purchase. They probably thought I wanted a drink, too.

Sam returned from his walk and started playing alongside me. Sometimes our playing was still so off that money was more likely to come from people who regretted our musicianship than our homelessness. That night, though, we were *on*. Our music was loud and strong, and in just half an hour we pulled in nearly ten dollars. It was more than enough to buy dinner at our favorite Mexican restaurant just up the street.

Sam and I were talking about taking our cash that way when an old man came riding along in an electric wheelchair. He was yelling and cussing at everything he passed, including pedestrians, dogs, garbage cans, and stoplights. He wore dark sunglasses and no shirt, and his long white hair and beard flowed softly behind him as he motored toward us. Off the back of his chair hung a cluster of white plastic bags.

Right in front of me, he braked with a screech. "Plug me in, sonny!" he commanded loudly, looking down from his perch.

I looked around, unsure what he wanted plugged in, or where.

"Here!" He held out a black, badly worn plug. It was the

recharge cord for his chair. "Shove it right there in the wall behind your pack!"

Sure enough, behind my pack I found the outlet and plugged him in, hoping not to electrocute myself on the frayed wiring. Meanwhile, Sam stood up to introduce himself.

"I'm Sam," he said, offering his hand.

"Ronnie!" the old man yelled.

"Mike," I said, standing up, too.

"Delighted!" Ronnie yelled.

"You're all set to go," I said, pointing to the wall.

"Thank you, sonny!" he said. "Now, if you'll just let me see that there guitar, we'll all have a grand old time!" And he reached for my guitar.

Well, I was tired of playing anyway, so I handed it to him. Whatever song he chose, I fully expected Ronnie to yell his way through every word.

He gave the guitar a spin, and began to play and sing. Amazingly, Ronnie could belt out a song at high volume and still sound terrific. He played one Rolling Stones song after another, and Sam and I just sat back and took it in. Others began to gather and clap along. Between songs, Ronnie would pause to thank his audience, especially those who had dropped dollar bills into my case. After five studio-quality covers, Ronnie gave the guitar another spin and handed it back.

"Thank you, boys!" he shouted. "I think I'm all charged up now!"

Reaching down he grabbed the cord and gave it a yank. Then slinging the cord over his shoulder, he punched a lever on his chair and shot forward. Sam and I jumped to get out of his way, and he disappeared up the avenue.

When the crowd had dispersed, we sat down, keenly

aware that whatever we played next—even if it was our best—would never come close to Wheelchair Ronnie.

"Does that make you want to play more or less?" Sam asked.

"What do you mean?"

"Sometimes good players make me want to play better," he said, "make me want to practice more. But sometimes they make me want to give up 'cause I know I'll never be that good."

I thought for a minute. "Well, a musician like Ronnie would usually make me want to play better. But not tonight," I said. "I don't feel like playing this guitar anymore, period. It's kind of like McDonald's. If I never eat another ninety-nine-cent hamburger, I won't consider it a disappointment."

- - -

183

Just then a tall, skinny man came up the street, moving quickly and glancing back over his shoulder. His sweatshirt and holey jeans were badly stained. His face looked more like a skull than an actual living human being—high cheek bones, tightly stretched skin, and eyes sunk deeply back into their sockets.

As he got up to us, he glared behind him at the empty street and screamed, "I'm gonna kill you! I'm gonna kill you, man!"

"Whoa, whoa, whoa!" I said as he neared, hoping to calm him down.

He stopped. "What do you want?" he shouted, staring me down.

"I just don't want anyone to get killed today," I said, nodding in the direction he'd just come.

Suddenly, his mood seemed to change. "Hey, can I play your guitar?" he asked, and sat down next to Sam.

"Sure," Sam said, handing him his guitar with a shrug. Looked like we might be in for another concert from another Old Yeller.

"Thanks. I'm Andrew," he said and held out a hand to both of us. At least he had stopped shouting.

Again the street filled with song. And wouldn't you know it, Andrew played even better than Ronnie, and had a bigger repertoire. From the Beatles to the Monkees, Led Zeppelin to the Stones, on and on he played. More people stopped to listen, impressed by Andrew's guitar mastery and clear voice. Then, just as abruptly as he had started, Andrew quit, thanked Sam, handed back his guitar, and jumped up to leave.

"Hey wait, Andrew." I yelled. "You hungry?"

The question made Andrew pause, and he turned around. "I'm starving," he said.

He held up a thin hand. "I haven't eaten in one, two, three, four days," he said, counting off the days one bony finger at a time. "Why do you ask?"

I grabbed some of the crumpled dollars from the guitar case and looked up the street. "We were just going to buy some dinner up there," I said. "Come on. We'll get you something, too."

"You serious?" Andrew said with disbelief, walking slowly back toward us.

"You bet, bro," said Sam. "There's a great Mexican shop just up the street. Burritos and flautas there are like one seventy-five each. We'll totally hook you up."

"Oh man, oh man," Andrew said, getting excited. "I spent all of my money today on alcohol and speed. Thanks, you guys. Thanks."

Sam agreed to watch the packs and guitars while Andrew and I walked up the street. Andrew was so excited he nearly ran in front of me. At the restaurant, Andrew ordered the largest burrito, everything on it. I bought two flautas. Dinner for three homeless men added up to seven bucks.

As we headed back, Andrew dug in. Through huge mouthfuls, with sour cream and guacamole all over his face, he kept thanking me. "You have no idea, man. No idea. This is amazing. I didn't think I was going to eat for another couple days."

"Why is that?" I asked.

"Gotta have my speed, man!" he said with an odd grin. The certainty in his voice was chilling.

I had to ask another question. "Why are you down here on the streets, Andrew. I mean, the way you can play and sing, you could be a signed artist."

He swallowed, looking frustrated. "I know. Believe me, I know," he said. "I was, in fact. Then somebody, my *partner*"— he spat out the word with enormous disgust—"screwed me and took my money." With that he suddenly spun to the left and sprinted across the street, nearly getting hit by a car.

When I got back to Sam, I handed him the brown paper bag containing dinner. Then, leaning up against the liquor store, we prayed over our meal and dug in.

"Where's Andrew?" Sam asked.

"Did you hear that car horn up the road?"

"Yeah."

"That was Andrew. A car was barreling right down on top of him and he didn't even care. Interesting guy. Lot of problems."

"Yeah, seemed like it," said Sam quietly. "I like him, though."

- - -

A few nights later Sam and I sat playing on a street corner, hoping to earn enough for another meal at the Mexican restaurant.

It was a slow evening, maybe because a bagpipe player had taken our normal spot by the liquor store. Even though we were set up three blocks away, his shrill piping seemed to dominate the street.

Sam set down his guitar and looked glumly at the few coins in our case. "Not going too well," he said.

"Nope," I said. "A few months ago, I would have been discouraged, but meager earnings were a normal part of street life. Feelings of helplessness just came with the territory."

Suddenly, Andrew came walking along, hands in pockets, deeply slouched. His demeanor was entirely different than it had been a few nights earlier. He walked slowly and with determination. "Hey, boys," he said softly, and sat down next to us.

"Hey, Andrew. Want to play?" I asked, offering my guitar.

"Naw! I like Sam's better," Andrew said, reaching for Sam's guitar. He opened with a Beatles song. It didn't take long for his voice and the beat of the guitar to drown out the sounds of the bagpipe down the street. And the responsiveness of passersby was amazing to watch. Whereas they'd sometimes cross to the other side of the street to avoid us, tonight they'd cross the street just to stand and listen to Andrew play. An older man and his wife dressed for an evening on the town actually sat down next to us and began swaying slowly back and forth, eyes closed, engulfed in the music. At one point, about ten people were gathered in a circle around Andrew, some drinking, some smoking, all loving the music.

Andrew paused for a moment, the guitar still echoing, and looked from Sam to me and back again. "I love this!" he said. And he burst into another song that brought a cheer from his fans.

An hour later, Andrew broke a string. He kept playing, but when he'd finished the song, he hopped up and said his show was over. As people began to depart, Andrew grabbed a handful out of the collection of dollar bills and fives that had gathered in our case.

"Keep the rest," he said blankly, and headed off. He was already focused on something else.

"You sure?" Sam called after him.

"Yeah," Andrew said, not looking back. "It's your guitar, right?"

"Keep it clean, Andrew," I yelled after him. It was futile, of course, and I had a sinking feeling that we had somehow become part of sustaining Andrew's drug habit.

Sam and I collected our things, and walked down to the end of the street, where a small park overlooked the ocean. When we got there, I watched the gear while Sam walked to buy more of our favorite flautas.

Just as Sam got back with dinner, two new guys in dress clothes stopped to talk with us. While Sam and I ate, we found out more about one another. The two men belonged to a local church and were beginning a community outreach, and so had decided to spend some time hanging out "with the people." We explained to them where most of the homeless slept—over by the cliffs or down the beach.

We had been talking for about half an hour when we heard a loud "Yee haw!" Here came Andrew, parading down the center of the street, arms open wide, coffee in one hand, cigarette in the other. He was yelling and singing and shaking his head from side to side as though trying to knock something away. Even from a distance I could see a wild gleam in his eyes. He walked at a frantic pace, as if someone had shortened the length of a second and Andrew was hurrying to catch up.

"Who's that?" one of the church guys asked. Before Sam or I could manage an explanation, Andrew headed directly toward us. But when he reached us, he kept right on walking, yelling and laughing wildly, staring out into the Pacific. Then he spun around, marched back, and threw his arms around me and one of the church guys, spilling some of the coffee on the man's white shirt. Although the man jumped backward, his shirt steaming in the cold night air, Andrew didn't notice.

"I'm Andrew!" he yelled. Then he faced the new guys. "And who are you?"

"Mark," said the one with the coffee on his shirt.

"Steve," said the other.

Both extended their hands, but Andrew didn't shake. Instead he slapped them on the back, one after the other, spilling more steaming coffee. "You friends with these guys?" Andrew asked Steve, pointing at Sam and me.

"Getting to be."

"Good! So what's new?" Andrew asked, then without waiting for an answer, walked away. Turning back toward us, laughing, yelling, and continuously rolling his head, Andrew appeared nonsensical. What with his frantic movements, high-pitched voice, and bizarre behavior, his presence was entirely unnerving.

Back in front of us now, he paused, thinking. He took a sip of his coffee, and with a quick flip of his thumb, popped the plastic lid off his cup. It fell to the cement. Then with a wink in our general direction, he lifted the steaming cup and poured all the coffee on his head. He closed his eyes as it ran down his face and neck. Obviously, the coffee was scalding his chest and back, but he seemed oblivious.

When he opened his eyes, he looked at us numbly and said in a barely audible voice, "Have a great evening."

Then he took off at a trot down the center of the street, head back, yelling the whole way.

"Is he okay?" Steve asked, not sure what else to do.

"Let's just say it's a good thing you guys are here," I said, watching Andrew disappear.

We spent about another hour sharing with Mark and Steve some of our perspective about life on the streets, excited that they felt called to be in the thick of the madness. By that point in our journey it seemed we had more than enough perspective to go around.

As we talked, the four of us agreed on one thing: Yes, God is alive and well on the streets of America, but so is Satan...

He is busy stealing talents from promising lives.

He is breaking bodies and smashing dreams.

He is locking up good minds behind the bars of addiction.

He is trading in the music of God for the sound of a crazy man yelling his head off in the middle of the street, destruction barreling straight at him.

CIRCLE OF LIGHT

I was in the middle of playing solo in front of the liquor store when a guy in his fifties came up, dropped his enormous pack with a thud, and took a seat next to us. Then he grabbed a darkly stained blue hat off his head, placed it brim-up just in front of him, and dropped in a few coins.

"Grow baby, grow!" he said sarcastically toward his hat.

Looking across the gap between us he asked with a toothless smile, "Mind if I sit here for a while with you?"

With one final strum I ended my song and looked over at him. "Not at all!"

His name was Doug. He smelled pretty bad. Even his blue hat smelled. I guess he wanted me to play while he watched his money grow, but I didn't mind.

"Are you going to play anymore tonight?" Doug asked after a couple minutes of silence.

"You bet. I was just resting my fingers for a while," I answered, picking up my guitar and beginning to play a familiar worship song. After the first verse, Doug leaned over and broke in with an excited whisper. "Are you a Christian?"

"That I am," I said.

"You're a Christian," Doug mumbled to himself. "You're a Christian?" Doug asked again with unmasked suspicion.

"Yes, I am. Are you?" I responded.

"Yes, I am," he said. Then he seemed to shrink as he added, "At least I try to be."

Just then Sam returned from his evening walk around Ocean Beach and sat down next to Doug.

"Hey, guys!" he said, looking between Doug and me. As he reached out his hand to Doug, the older man looked amazed.

"Are you a Christian, too?" he asked.

"Yes, I am," Sam said, shaking Doug's hand.

"Is he a Christian, too?" Doug asked me, looking back over at me. He was pointing at Sam in disbelief.

"Yes, he's a Christian, too."

Doug sank into thought for a moment. Then he exclaimed, "This is amazing! I can't believe it! I've run into more Christians in the past two days than I did the whole last month. It's like

God is trying to help me, because I keep asking Him for help! Your being here is God's being here!"

As we talked, we learned that Doug had lived on the streets since his return from the Vietnam War. While he was describing his fighting experiences, he sat up straight. Once he saluted the memory. But as he began talking about his years-long struggle with alcoholism, drugs, and depression, he seemed to sink lower and lower.

Sam and I were about to start playing again when Doug spoke up with a request. "Hey, do you guys know how to play the song about the deer?"

"You mean 'As the Deer'?"

"Yeah!" Doug said with enthusiasm. "That's my favorite song. Can we sing it?"

"Definitely."

It must have made for an odd scene: three grimy men sitting on the sidewalk outside a liquor store panhandling to a psalm of longing for God.

> *As the deer panteth for the water*
> *So my soul longeth after Thee*
> *You alone are my heart's desire*
> *And I long to worship Thee*

Our three voices rose and wavered together in awkward unison. People walking by stared, while we put our hearts into the prayer. We really did long for God. But after months on the streets—years for Doug—it was a longing that felt like a knife in the heart.

As we finished, Doug began to weep. Soon he was racked with sobs. Sam and I looked at each other, not sure of what to do next.

"You okay, Doug?" I asked, putting a hand on his shoulder.

"Yeah," he said, wiping at his eyes. "It's just that I try to be a good Christian. I try to give glory to the Lord. But I just fall so much." He dropped his head and began to shake again. "I mean, we're singing worship songs and I'm collecting money for a drink before I go to sleep tonight."

We tried to encourage him. "When you become a Christian," I said, "God promised to come into your life and make you new. You can trust Him in that."

"Oh, I know," said Doug, and let out a deep sigh. "I used to be addicted to cocaine and acid and I slept around all the time but God has helped me in all of those things. I haven't used drugs in over ten years. But I still get drunk every day."

Sam spoke up. "You just told us that God was faithful in helping you overcome your addictions to drugs, right?"

Doug agreed, not sure of where the conversation was going.

"Then you can trust Him enough to believe that He is ready to help you with your alcoholism, too," said Sam.

"But why can't He just change me in an instant? He did that to people in the Bible. BAM! They were changed. Why doesn't He just change me? I want to be good and stop sinning! Why won't He change me?" Doug's tone rose to a whine.

While customers for the liquor store came and went, we shared Bible verses with Doug. We encouraged him to see that he had a part, too, in his own deliverance—that his daily decisions could either help or hinder God.

When he had cheered up, Doug stood and grabbed his pack. "Will you guys please pray for me?" he asked.

We told him we would.

"I'll see you guys later, I hope," he said, and walked off down the street toward the ocean.

- - -

When Sam and I saw Doug two nights later, he seemed pretty out of it, and so did the friend he was sitting with. We were hanging out along a short wall overlooking the beach and the ocean. A flag above us flapped lazily in the night wind. People around us talked and smoked. Everyone was homeless, and some were drunk.

Sam and I were trying to make dinner with tortillas and peanut butter. The combination wasn't much to our liking, but for less than four dollars we could eat for a week. We only had one pack of tortillas left, though—the previous night while we slept at the cliffs, rats had devoured the other.

Two policemen rode slowly past all of us on bicycles, eyeing our group with obvious suspicion. They rode up one block, then came back to stop and get off their bikes directly in front of Doug and the other guy.

"Uh-oh," I said. The police seemed most interested in the man next to Doug. After a minute, Doug rose and slowly walked away toward us.

"This is not good," he said as he reached us and sat down. Sam made him a peanut butter tortilla, and Doug started eating, but he wasn't taking his eyes off the police. "Not good at all," Doug said again through a mouthful of peanut butter.

We watched as the police stood the man up next to the little wall, searched him, and put him in handcuffs. The whole while, they drilled him with questions, but he kept shaking his head silently.

One of the officers took a step backward and got in an intense conversation on his radio. The other suspiciously scanned the group of us clustered along the wall.

Suddenly the man with the handcuffs on flipped himself backward over the wall, landing on the sand about six feet below, and took off running toward the ocean with a yell. Both police jumped down to the sand and gave chase.

"Not good at all," Doug said again, turning to watch the men as they ran.

Within a minute the man had reached the water, but he kept on running, getting pummeled by the waves.

"He can't swim with handcuffs on!" Doug yelled.

Three squad cars pulled up, red and blue lights flashing, and more officers joined in the chase. They pointed powerful search lights at the fugitive, now a tiny black spot out in the surf.

More onlookers gathered, yelling and cursing. Everybody seemed to find the chase the perfect entertainment. Some screamed at the guy to come back. Some told him to swim until he got to Japan.

Then a police helicopter arrived overhead, its rotors thumping ominously as it headed out to sea where it hovered over the scene, flooding the figure in the water in a brilliant circle of light.

Doug was getting increasingly anxious. "He's going to drown and nobody's doing anything!" he shouted. "He's going to drown!" Doug was nearly in tears. Suddenly he, too, leaped off the wall and began running, hands held high, toward the commotion.

When he reached the police at the water's edge, he stopped to talk for a while, then proceeded alone out into the water. The closer he got to his friend, the more the waves crashed around him. Soon they were two dots bobbing in the water.

The crowd along the wall settled in to watch the drama

194

unfold. All eyes were on the shining circle of light, in the center of which two men now stood shouting back and forth. Police stood by in the sand, and the chopper roared overhead.

After about ten minutes of a standoff, we could see Doug walk closer to the other man, and then they both turned and began making the way back to shore.

Doug was greeted back at the wall with cheers and applause. The guy in handcuffs left in a squad car. Police turned off their searchlights and melted away in the night, and so did the chopper. Soon the scene along the sea wall looked as though nothing at all had happened.

- - -

"I couldn't just stand there and watch him drown," Doug was saying as he dried himself off with a filthy towel from his backpack. He was still breathing heavily. "It's like when Jesus came in after me when I was drowning. I had to go in after him."

"You did really well, Doug," Sam said, handing him another tortilla. We asked him what the arrest had been about.

Doug shook his head, sending a spray of water over Sam and me. "I don't know. He shouldn't have run, though. Not a good idea." We all sat in silence for a while, looking out to the ocean.

Then Doug began to weep again, his shoulders convulsing.

"You okay, Doug?" I asked.

"Oh, yeah," Doug said, between sobs. "It's just so hard for me to live like a Christian. I've been drunk all day. I just hate that. Why can I be so evil one minute and then so good another? I just saved a guy and this morning I was so drunk I couldn't stand. Jesus, forgive me!"

Then, standing upon the wall still dripping, he yelled up to the black sky, "Why won't You just fix me?"

With tears still streaming, Doug climbed back down, grabbed his pack and walked off, chewing on the tortilla.

"You about ready to sleep?" Sam asked.

"Yeah, all this craziness is tiring."

We grabbed our packs, said good night to the people still hanging around, and walked off into the night.

- - -

It was only about a five minute walk down the sidewalk past a dimly lit parking lot to the cliffs where we slept every night. Our spot was a sandy area between an apartment building and the ocean. We stretched out our sleeping bags and strapped our guitars to our packs. I put the bag with the tortillas in it next to my head so if the rats returned, I'd hear them.

Lying there in our bags listening to the waves, we talked about Doug. His brokenness about his sins was convincing. "I wish my sin pained me as greatly as Doug's does," said Sam.

"Would you do anything about it if it did?" I asked.

"What do you mean?" Sam asked, sounding sleepy.

"Doug longs to be cleansed and free of his sins, but I don't know. I don't think he's willing to stop doing the very thing that grieves him. Walking over here tonight, I was wondering if there are things in my life that I am praying for deliverance from but refuse let go of. It's a scary thought."

Few of the men and women we'd met on the streets had arrived there suddenly. Most had gotten there by a series of choices, a gradual, willful progression along a downward slope. One day you end up, like Doug, on the other side of the Grand Canyon from the life you desperately want.

As I drifted off, I could still see Doug out there on the sand, hands high, running out into the waves to save his friend. How much I longed for Jesus to come and save our friend. "Find Doug out there in the waves," I prayed. "Keep him fixed in Your circle of light."

FREEDOM RINGS

One evening, Doug introduced us to Rings, a kindhearted old chain smoker who lived in the cab of his pickup truck. Doug wanted to show off his other Christian friend. "Rings is the best Christian man in the world," he said proudly.

When Rings heard that we, too, were believers, he was excited.

"You guys are an answer to my prayers," he said. "Do you know that?"

"How?" Sam asked.

"I've been told by God to feed the homeless in this town," he said through a cloud of smoke. "Heck, I'm homeless and He feeds me, so I feed others. But I'm getting too old and tired. I needed some help, so I prayed, and along came you two!"

When Rings got too excited, his chest would start rattling, then he'd roll into a round of deep coughing. If the bout went on long enough, he'd start cursing under his breath.

"Pretty amazing how God works," I said, while he recovered. Sam and I were happy to meet Rings, too. With the exception of Doug, we hadn't met many Christians on the streets recently.

Over the next minutes, Rings told us about his personal feeding program and invited us to help him out the next day.

197

We said yes, and agreed to meet at 6:30 A.M. for coffee.

As Rings left to sleep in his truck, a tear rolled down Doug's cheek. "That man gives me hope," Doug said, wiping his cheek with a dirty hand. "He's dry. He used to be a heavier drinker than me but he's dry now. Jesus sobered him up, just like I want Him to sober me up."

Doug walked away mumbling a prayer. Sam and I headed for the cliffs for the night.

- - -

The next morning, Rings didn't arrive until almost 7:30. But we didn't mind. Waking up in a truck cab every morning at his age was probably taking its toll. So we waited.

Rings couldn't even talk until he had downed two cups of coffee and smoked his way through three cigarettes. We waited some more.

Finally, after an intense bout of coughing, Rings looked up with a twinkle in his eye.

"Well, boys," he said. "Like I told you, you're the answer to my prayers. I got a check yesterday, and my coolers are all empty in the back of my truck. When we finish our coffee, we'll go to the store and buy enough food to cook up a feast. The folks down at the park will be speechless!"

This last thought gave him so much obvious pleasure, he started to laugh, and that led to more coughing, and eventually to more cursing.

I was impressed that a guy living in a truck cab would consistently give his entire (measly) government check to feed others in similar straits. Most homeless people we'd met blew their checks on booze and drugs within a couple of days.

I gave him time to regain his composure. "Rings, who are you, *really?*" I asked.

"I'm just a man," Rings said with a wink. "Jesus saved me. Been a trucker, a carnie, a door-to-door salesman, a husband, a father. I've been in jail, been an addict, been a drunk. Now I follow Christ. All that I have is His. If He can save me, He can save anybody."

We asked him to tell us more, but Rings had other plans. "It's been a crazy road, that's for sure," he said. "But come on— the road up ahead is always better than the road behind. Let's get started."

With that, he finished a last swallow of coffee and jumped up from the table.

We walked out to his battered pickup, piled in, and drove off to a nearby supermarket. There we bought a hundred dollars' worth of eggs, milk, orange juice, pancake mix, steak, tortillas, and butter. Then we headed for the beach.

199

- - -

Jesus fed thousands with a boy's lunch. What a sight that must have been!

Rings fed twenty or so that day out of the back of his truck. And what a sight that was, too. Hungry, forgotten people stood around in a circle in the foggy morning air watching an old man hunched over his propane stove cooking and smoking, cooking and smoking. I don't think an eye ever left the chef's hands as he worked.

A few cigarette ashes floated down on the food. "A little seasoning," Rings pronounced. "That's all, a little seasoning." I looked at Sam and we both shrugged. After surviving for a couple of weeks on corn tortillas and peanut butter, Rings' culinary creation smelled to us like a million dollars.

When the tailgate feast was ready, and the first man stepped up to take his plate, Rings had a speech ready.

"Do you know why I do this?" he asked his attentive audience. "I do this because Christ pulled me out of the mess I was in. Then He told me to do this. You want to be free? This is freedom! Enjoy!"

And breakfast was served.

ASHES AND SNOW

I sat up coughing, my eyes burning, my head feeling as heavy and thick as a brick. In the footprints in the sand near where we'd been sleeping, snowflakes lifted and swirled in a light breeze.

But wait a minute! This was San Diego, and I was hot in my sleeping bag.

I stared at the swirling flakes for a while—stared with that really dumb stare a just-awakened person has where what you're looking at is probably not what you're seeing.

Then I smelled fire. The swirling particles all around me were soot and ash, not snow, and the air was filled with smoke. The sky above us was not its usual deep-sea blue, but brown. Over the mountains to the east, a blood-red sun showed faintly through the haze. Next to me, Sam was still asleep in his bag. The white ash in his hair made him look ancient.

I shook him awake. He looked around. "Dude!" he blurted. "Is the city on fire?"

"Looks like it, bud," I said. "Come on, we need to go."

Once out on the street, we learned that a fire had begun the previous day, Saturday, in a canyon just east of the city.

High winds had fanned the blaze into a firestorm, consuming thousands of acres blanketing much of greater San Diego in smoke and ash. People lucky enough to have a house could close their windows, turn on air purifiers, and crank up air conditioners. For those of us who lived out-of-doors, a wet bandanna over nose and mouth would have to do.

Ocean Beach seemed nearly vacant, and we wondered where we could find a refuge for a few hours until we went to church. We ended up passing time in a Starbucks, much to the frustration of some of the workers.

At about nine o'clock we started walking through the gloomy streets toward the church.

As we walked I thought of how different my life was now from what it had been less than a year before. I could hardly see a bridge anymore between that existence and my present one. That former world seemed more like a movie I'd seen once than my actual past. Our daily cycle—waking up to panhandle, panhandling to eat, and eating to sleep—seemed pathetic in the extreme.

Did anyone back home really care that last night we slept on a stretch of sand where the rats weren't as bad? That hamburgers on Tuesdays are cheaper on 6th Street than on 9th? That what looked like snow here was actually ash, and it was burning in our throats?

Maybe it was the heavy brooding sky that had turned my thoughts so dark. Or maybe it was the wear and tear of five months living from hand to mouth on the cement.

As we walked, we kicked up white ashes from the fire. Watching it swirl around my feet I couldn't help thinking of the clean, cool snows of my Colorado home.

Inside the church, clusters of mostly older folks stood

around discussing the fire, too taken up with the news to notice a couple of bums joining them for worship. Sam and I found a pew directly underneath an air vent. A steady stream of cool, clean air had never felt more refreshing (although I felt sympathy for everyone downwind of us).

The simple service was in honor of the church's first pastor, who was retiring that day. Although there was frequent applause, my head drooped in exhaustion. I jerked to immediate attention though when the new pastor invited everyone to a potluck in honor of his predecessor. Sam and I looked at each other like we'd just fallen into Betty Crocker's kitchen.

We followed the congregation to an upstairs gymnasium where we found long tables crammed with delicious-looking homemade food. When a petite, white-haired woman saw us enter the room, she walked right over. She gazed up at us with honest delight. "I'm *so* glad you two decided to stay for the potluck," she said. "I'm Carla. We've got lots of food here, so come on, grab a seat, and we'll start in just a couple of minutes. What are your names?"

We told her as she marched us to a table, where she loudly proclaimed, "Folks, these are my new friends, Sam and Mike. George, move over and make room for these big boys. I want you to make them feel right at home!" And George did, along with the rest of our slightly startled tablemates.

They say that in Jesus' time, eating together was one of the greatest signs of friendship, honor, and acceptance. For Sam and me, that church potluck on a smoky day in San Diego was a feast of all of the above—home-cooked love included.

What would happen, I wondered, if two rank, homeless strangers like Sam and I wandered in to enjoy the air-conditioning at my church back home? Good things, I hoped, but

202

I wasn't so sure anymore. The months of rejection by church after church had given me my doubts. Regular church attenders tend to come to our places of worship to feel better, not to be hit with the unfamiliar, the uncomfortable, the threatening.

That's what made the afternoon potluck so spectacular. Carla kept coming over to make sure her two rank, homeless strangers were getting enough food and friendliness. We were. I followed her puff of white hair as she floated around the room taking care of everyone. I'm not sure she ever sat down to eat herself.

Sitting there at peace, I thought back to how much life on the road had changed my view of aging, of church, of service in Jesus' name. How much it had changed my praying, too. I tried to recall typical prayers from the previous summer. Let's see, probably: *Lord, help me get my Land Cruiser fixed. Lord, help that professor see that I really do deserve an A. Lord, help my plans come together. Lord, give me....*

203

But so much of that Mike seemed to have disappeared. Just yesterday, for example, my prayers had been of a different nature altogether: for a meal (*at least one, Lord*), for a place to sleep (*not too many rats*), for the guy whose girlfriend left a seven-inch gash across his back with a switchblade (*may it not get infected*), for the girlfriend (*show her Your tenderness, Lord*).

Ashes and snow.

Sam and I were going home soon, leaving one world and returning to another. But we would not go back unchanged. Some things had burned up, and we'd leave them behind to blow away on the wind. Other things we would take into our futures, and those few things were pure and precious and true.

The ashes and snow were swirling together.

COMING BACK
TO NORMAL

At 8:00 P.M. on November 2nd, it was all over. Justin, a friend from Sam's hometown, picked us up outside the public library in Ocean Beach to take us out for a celebration dinner. But first, he drove us to his apartment to clean up. Before we stepped back into our other world, we needed to wash away the filth of street life.

I weighed myself. I had lost twenty-five pounds.

I turned the shower on all the way to hot and watched as the bathroom began to fill with steam. A worn and filthy man just in off the streets stared back at me from the mirror. I made a mental inventory: scraggly beard, matted hair with bits and pieces of several destinations embedded in the dreadlocks, dark circles under the eyes, a ring of filth around the neck, grime pressed into the creases of the skin, sun-baked arms and face and neck...

I didn't want to forget this person I'd chosen to become.

Then steam moved over the glass and the homeless man was gone.

I stepped into the shower, grateful for its warmth on my aching body. Grateful for my privacy, too—this was my first shower in ages without a dozen other naked, dirty men crowding into the group showers at the rescue missions.

The water ran through my hair and beard and over my body, and when it ran down the drain, it ran almost black. I scrubbed with soap, and shampooed and rinsed. Then I started over. After the third go-round, the water still ran murky around my feet. Maybe the evidences of my street life were going to take more time to wash away than I'd thought.

When I dried myself on a clean white towel, the towel turned dingy. The next round of cleaning would have to wait. At least I couldn't smell myself anymore. I let out a sigh and walked out into the bedroom.

A box of clothes from my previous life waited for me on the bed. My family had sent them so I would have something to change into when this moment arrived. The clothes felt strange and stiff as I unfolded and put them on. The whiteness of the T-shirt seemed unreal—for so long the brightest white I had known was just another shade of gray.

- - -

For our big dinner, we decided to go to P. F. Chang's for Chinese food. On the way to the restaurant, it started to rain, thick drops splatting against the windshield.

"We're finished," Sam said, grabbing my shoulder. He didn't sound like he actually believed it.

"Yeah," I said. I tapped the wet window. "No more living out in that stuff."

"Nope."

We drove in silence for a minute. Then Sam said, "I wonder how Bob, Doug, Rings, and Andrew are doing?"

More silence.

After we'd ordered at the restaurant, I turned to Sam. "I still feel like we're going to sleep next to the cliffs by the beach tonight." I was having trouble grasping our new circumstances, too.

"Yeah, I know," he said.

When our food arrived, we gave a heartfelt thanks and dug in. The table was crowded with four main dishes, Cashew Chicken, Honey Chicken, Mongolian Beef, and Chow Mein, each piled high and steaming. The tastes and smells were so rich and inviting, and yet completely foreign at the same time. I felt like we were indulging in some forgotten joy and had to relearn how to appreciate it.

"Hey, watch this," I said to Sam. Raising my empty water glass, I caught the server's attention and she hurried over with a full pitcher. "Amazing, huh?" I said as she filled my glass along with Sam's.

"Yep," Sam said as she walked away. "I'd forgotten it was that easy. No more two-mile walks for water!"

Later that night we returned to Justin's apartment. Both Sam and I were ready to crash. We said good night after just a few short minutes of conversation, and each went to separate rooms.

I had a bed to sleep in.

With the exception of the sunken, creaky bunks at the rescue missions with eighty other men snoring in the same room, this was my first bed since May twenty-sixth.

I climbed in between the clean sheets, switched off the light, and let out a happy sigh. No more three-dollar sleeping bags. No more security guards, rain, or rats. I was certain I'd fall right to sleep.

About an hour later, though, I was still awake. I rolled over and looked at the clock. It was 11:27. Frustrated and exhausted, I tossed and turned.

At 12:15, I sat up, unsure of what to do. The room was just so *quiet*. There were no sounds of traffic, no horns, no people walking past, no drunks shouting, no winds in the eucalyptus, no rollers breaking across the sand. Above my head, where there had been stars or fog or trees or buildings for so many months, I saw only a white ceiling. And around me, instead of concrete or bushes, only four warm walls.

Unaccountably, I felt alone, somehow cut off from the rest of human life.

But you're comfortable..., I thought to myself.

"Are you?" I asked out loud. "Then why can't you fall asleep?"

Being uncomfortable with comfort wasn't something I had expected to come home to.

208

WANTING MORE (AND MORE)

On our way up to my college's campus in Santa Barbara, Sam and I stopped into a bookstore. Having spent so much time during our travels in libraries, we hoped that being back in a familiar environment would help us to capture our feelings and observations in our journals.

The familiar feelings proved elusive, though. In their place was a new, stronger feeling. I hadn't felt it in a while. I wanted to *consume*—to have, to own, to buy. Not because I needed anything, mind you, but because now I could.

As I walked around the store, things I would never have thought beneficial or desirable suddenly jumped out at me.

With every lap around the rows of stuff, my wish list grew: books, books, and more books; magazines; leather bound journals; nice pens; expensive maps…

Finally I plopped down in a chair across from Sam. He put aside his journal.

"What's up?" he asked.

"I'd buy this whole store if I could. Right now. Even the stuff I don't want. Just because I can."

"Huh. That's kinda dumb."

"Yeah, isn't it weird? Just because I ate breakfast this morning and slept in a bed last night and I'm wearing nice clothes and have the options at my fingertips, I want to indulge. I've been away from all the good stuff for so long, and dang-it, now I want it!"

"Yeah, I feel it, too," said Sam. "Like that globe over there by the door. I've never had a globe, never thought about owning one, but when I walked in, I thought, 'It'd be nice to have that.'"

"We're going to have to be careful," I said. I told him about a part I remembered from *The Count of Monte Cristo* where a character warns that sailors have to be careful after they're rescued from a shipwreck or they'll eat so much their stomach's will burst.

"Do you think two years from now we'll still be wanting more, more, more?" Sam asked.

We talked about that for a while. We didn't want to give in to our feast-till-we-burst reflex now that we were back. We wanted the good changes to remain. We wanted to live in plenty but remember the sharp lessons of living in want.

"Check out this verse I read this morning," I said to Sam, and pointed him to Deuteronomy 8:7–11.

> *"For the LORD your God is bringing you into a*
> *good land—a land with streams and pools of water,*
> *with springs flowing in the valleys and hills; a land*
> *with wheat and barley, vines and fig trees, pome-*
> *granates, olive oil and honey; a land where bread*
> *will not be scarce and you will lack nothing. . . .*
> *When you have eaten and are satisfied, praise the*
> *LORD your God for the good land he has given*
> *you. Be careful that you do not forget the LORD*
> *your God."*

Suddenly the terrible dangers of lacking nothing came clear to us. Having everything "just because you can" is a trap. It numbs and blinds the human spirit. It can separate us from our calling and our privilege as Christians in this needy world.

"Be careful that you do not forget..."

In the weeks after we returned, Sam and I talked often about that. Again and again it seemed that the culture we had returned to knew how to enjoy God's material blessings, but had forgotten—or didn't care to know—how to use those blessings to help others in Jesus' name.

We didn't want that to happen to us.

Ever.

STREET VISITOR

As I write this, it's been more than a year since Sam and I said good-bye to the streets and to the life that we had come to know there. We're back to "normal" life—consistent meals, clean clothes, our own beds, doors with locks, bathrooms. A couple of months after our return, Sam enrolled at Multnomah

Bible College in Portland, where he is a biblical studies major. "I am here to know and be known by my Lord—to be formed in Him," he told me recently. "It is the only adequate answer." I returned to Westmont College to pick up my education where I left off.

Actually, the transition back to college life took more time than we expected. We both did a lot of journaling, thinking, talking, praying. We sometimes wrestled with guilt about abandoning the homeless community and returning so easily to our former comforts. We struggled to understand how to put our experiences in the context of our other relationships and our career plans. Gratefully, our advisory group again played a huge role in that debriefing and adjusting period for each of us.

Outwardly, these days we look like any other college students. Inside, though, we constantly relive the sights, sounds, and smells of the street. We remember names and faces, and the stories they told. Sam and I talk about them and pray for them often. We still feel connected to the ragamuffin community of America's homeless.

One chilly evening after we'd returned, I found myself in downtown Denver on the streets again—this time as a visitor, not a resident. I encountered a young guy standing outside a restaurant with his hands in his pockets. As I neared him and made eye contact, he asked for spare change.

"What do you need the money for?" I asked, hoping to engage him a little bit.

"Bro, I'm just trying to get a piece of pizza," he replied, pointing to the restaurant sign above us.

"Well, I can't give you any money, but I would be more than happy to buy you a piece of pizza," I said. He eagerly accepted my offer, and together we walked inside.

211

While we waited for the pizza to arrive, I discovered he had recently come from San Diego. When I mentioned that I, too, had spent time on the streets there, he opened up a lot. We talked about familiar haunts, including Ocean Beach, but he didn't know anything of Andrew or Rings or Doug. Then his pizza arrived, he thanked me profusely, and we said our good-byes.

It was just a piece of pizza and a conversation, of course. But I prayed that God might have used me to encourage him. I know that for Sam and me, it was the simple kindnesses that brightened many dark days.

Not more than fifty feet from the pizza shop, I met a ragged, sun-weathered man stumbling along the sidewalk and singing. As I neared, he began yelling, "Give me a dollar!" He stumbled badly, righted himself with difficulty, then yelled, "I need a dollar for a beer before I go to sleep! Give me a dollar *now!*"

I stopped. "I'm not going to give you any money, man," I told him. "Not for beer. But if you're hungry, we can get some dinner."

"Yeah, whatever," he mumbled and staggered on his way.

The contrast between the two homeless men that evening highlighted for me one of the fundamental lessons I'd learned on the streets: We're responsible to help others toward hope in Jesus' name. But we're not responsible for their choices.

And I saw something else. For the rest of my life, there would always be that moment of recognition between me and a homeless person. A door in my heart would always stay open for my ragged brothers and sisters of the street. And I liked that.

NOW WHAT?

In a very real sense, the problem of homelessness is overwhelming. Jesus put it all in context when He said, "The poor you will have with you always." You just can't meet every need you see, or spend time with every homeless person you meet.

So where do we start? Jesus summarized right living in two powerful statements: "Love the Lord your God with all your heart...and love your neighbor as yourself." As over-spiritualized as it might sound, I really do think that caring for the needy begins with loving God more completely. It's in knowing and responding to His amazing love for us that we begin to set our priorities straight. Reflecting back on our trip, Sam put it this way: "Only in knowing God will we see people as they are, live as we were meant, and love as we were meant. Our relationship to Him didn't separate Mike and me from the needy and oppressed. Rather it pushed us closer to them. I think loving God is supposed to push all of us to be immersed in our world."

Fortunately, the "love your neighbor" part of Jesus' teaching starts with the simple actions and small opportunities that are available to each of us. Little things *do* mean a lot, especially in the kingdom of God, where giving a drink of cold water has eternal repercussions. And I am convinced that the more committed we become to impacting one person at a time—whether through a cup of coffee or a genuine conversation—the more we'll prepare our hearts and our churches to respond at both a community and national level.

The bottom line is that real love always shows itself in action. Nothing happens or changes in this world unless, by faith, we actually *do* something. So, with the needs of America's homeless in mind, here are a few ideas:

1. Find the rescue mission nearest to you. Call and find out how you can get involved. Show up an hour early and plan on leaving an hour after you're scheduled to. Have conversations with the homeless as they stand outside, waiting to get in. Bring bottled water, baked cookies, granola bars, patience, and a sense of humor. You'll bless those who cannot bless you in return.

2. Go downtown with a friend or friends (don't go alone). Buy cups of coffee or a bag of take-out food, find a homeless person sitting around asking for money, share your gifts, and enjoy a conversation. No agenda, no plans, no purpose other than to be with that person. You'll be amazed at what unfolds.

3. Is it cold outside? Go to your closet and grab the sweater, sweatshirt, or coat you keep telling your-self you'll wear sometime but know you won't. Call up four friends and tell them to do the same thing. Then go downtown and hand out your warm clothing to the men or women huddled under the overpass or in a doorway. As you stand there thinking of how cold your nose is, you'll be amazed at the genuine thankfulness of someone whose whole body is probably numb. And your giving will warm your soul, too.

4. Become a spokesperson in your youth group, church, and community for those who have no voice. Be relentlessly suspicious of your comfortable life, and of the comfort zones that render so many Christian fellowships insensitive and ineffective in our communities. God calls us all to more. And you and I can lead the way, one small step at a time.

But taking risks with your faith is about more than getting serious about homelessness. A radical choice to trust in the Lord must extend into all areas of your life, with everyone you encounter during your day. Which brings me to the larger message of this book.

215

THE RISK OF YOUR LIFE

What are the new steps of faith God is asking you to take today—steps that may feel like you're going off the edge of the known world for Him?

Who are the people God has placed in your life that He is calling you to notice, to reach out to, to share His love with?

My guess is you already know the answer to those questions. It's just that for most of us, acknowledging what we already know, and then acting on it takes more courage than we think we have. So we do nothing.

But that's leaving God out of the equation!

That first night on the streets of D.C., when it felt like Sam and I had dropped into oblivion, I prayed a desperate prayer: "Jesus, be our Rock." And He was. Even though the months brought more challenges than we could have imagined, even though we came to the end of ourselves again and again, Jesus held us safe in His power. And He will do the same for you, too.

What if following Him is hard? What if along the way He asks you to accomplish difficult tasks or to overcome intimidating obstacles? What if it requires more of you than you have to give?

Listen, that's the way it's supposed to be. Those places of need are where you and I discover ourselves, our faith, and—best of all—our God. It's there, in our weakness, that He shows Himself true, faithful, powerful, gracious, and loving.

God probably isn't calling you to live on the streets like He did Sam and me, but He *is* calling you—like He does each of His children—to take important risks of faith that are unique to you and your opportunities. I doubt those risks will have much to do with putting on a Christian acronym bracelet or a cross T-shirt. More likely, your journey will lead you toward utter dependence on the King of kings and a resolution to follow Him wherever He may ask you to go. That might be to the streets, to your friends and family, to your neighbor, or to a stranger you haven't even met yet.

Still not sure what your risk might be? Then I dare you to ask yourself a reality-rattling question: *What would I do during my day or in my life for God if I wasn't concerned with what I wear, what I eat, where I sleep, what I own, what people think of me, or what discomforts I face?* Think about your answer. You're probably at least in the neighborhood of where your personal journey starts.

If my question sounds a little over the edge, think of it as a rephrasing of the invitation Jesus presents to all His chosen ones:

216

Then Jesus said to his disciples, "If anyone would come after me, he must deny himself and take up his cross and follow me. For whoever wants to save his life will lose it, but whoever loses his life for me will find it." (Matthew 16:24–25)

The next step on a journey of faith always feels risky and a little scary. But it's also always terribly important and incredibly promising—and it's always up to us to take.

So join Sam and me and so many others in our generation. This Jesus we follow is the Redeemer of the world. This God we serve is the Rock on whom we stand. He's sure, steadfast, and worthy of our trust. He's calling us to live this life abandoned to Him, encouraged at all points by His Spirit and His Word and His people, looking to Him for all we need.

There's only this left to do:

Walk off the edge with Him.

217

EPILOGUE
TO THE UPDATED AND EXPANDED EDITION

FIVE YEARS ON

More than twenty people are seated around three small tables shoved together in a long, curving arc that stretches from the dining room into the middle of the living room. The table is heavy with food, and steam rises from the green beans as well as the mashed yams that lie invisible beneath a layer of golden marshmallows. It's Thanksgiving Day, 2009, and the intentional community home where my wife, Danae, and I live in Vancouver, B.C., is hosting a potluck Thanksgiving meal that would make even Julia Child's mouth water.

An interesting mix of people in their twenties, thirties, forties, and sixties anticipate the meal: refugees, homeless or formerly homeless people, recovering drug addicts and alcoholics, urban farmers, and even a few grad and undergrad students. All told, we've come from the United States, Canada, the United Kingdom, Germany, Australia, Colombia, Iraq, and Denmark. It's a mishmash of people, to be sure, and the gray and drippy Vancouver day has darkened most moods, some more than others. Nevertheless, we're glad to be together, and warmth has begun to seep back into us all.

Before we dig in, someone at the other end of the table begins the Doxology in a low, clear voice. I close my eyes, nearly moved to tears by what is happening. Surely this is a tiny and fleeting example of God's kingdom breaking into our broken world—people from so many different walks of life, so many socioeconomic positions, family backgrounds, religious backgrounds, educational backgrounds, drug backgrounds, housing backgrounds—all coming together in worship before breaking bread together. Other voices join in with the original singer, awkwardly harmonious and yet undeniably beautiful.

> Praise God, from whom all blessings flow!
> Praise Him, all creatures here below!
> Praise Him above, ye heavenly host!
> Praise Father, Son, and Holy Ghost!

The final "Amen" stretches on several seconds longer than usual, as though, despite our hunger, we all are yearning for the moment to last.

At last the room falls silent. We open our eyes…and feast.

- - -

Merriam-Webster defines *epilogue* as "a concluding section." By that definition, this shouldn't really be called an epilogue. After all, this journey of faith you've ventured on with Sam and me for the past two hundred pages or so certainly hasn't come to a conclusion.

It's hard to believe that it's been five years since *Under the Overpass* first came out. I'll try to bring you up to speed. Sam now lives in Portland, Oregon, where he is finishing up his degree in finance at Portland State University. His passion and occupation (a rare combination!) is coffee: buying, roasting, pulling espresso shots at a local shop, and teaching others how to do the same. Of course we still keep in touch and try to see each other whenever we're anywhere close by.

My wife, Danae, and I are grad students at Regent College. We dream of one day becoming an odd combination of small-holding farmers and college professors, with the hope of helping students consider the interplay between the Christian faith and Western culture and thus live into their vocations as creatures within a loving Creator's design.

As you glimpsed in the above snapshot, Danae and I recently lived in an intentional community on the east side of Vancouver. Our involvement in that living arrangement grew out of some of the things Sam and I learned on the streets: the need for active faith, the hope of hospitality in Jesus' name, and so on. This home is part of a group of community homes that individually and collectively seek to offer radical welcome in the name of Christ toward people who have barriers (mental, physical, chemical, financial, cultural) to living on their own.

I laugh as I reread the above sentence. It sounds wonderful. The reality, however, is anything but glamorous. In fact, it's really, *really* hard. This was our second community living situation, and Danae and I moved in having already had a good bit of our idealism about community life knocked out of us by our first experience. Nevertheless, community life was yet again far more difficult than we'd expected.

Don't get me wrong: there were moments of undeniable beauty and grace. Like the afternoon when one of the men in the house broke down weeping and thanked us for the way we welcomed him when he came through the front door every day. We didn't do anything dramatic, just called out,

"Hey, Simon! How was your day?" Through tears he told us that he'd never lived anyplace where people seemed glad when he came home.

But if there were moments of beauty and grace, there were hours and days of challenge. Some were intellectual, and we found ourselves asking tough questions: What does "hospitality" mean toward people who don't really seem to *want* hospitality? Can "community" happen without shared values? Does "community" mean anything more than just having the same address and sharing a meal every now and then? How can different understandings of personal hygiene and cleanliness coexist peacefully in the same shared space?

Other challenges were fiercely practical: How can you lovingly prevent someone who suffers with mental illness from dictating the mood of the entire house? What do you do when you have to study for a final exam the next day and the homeless man living in your basement is drunk and wants to talk? What does "gainful employment" mean for someone who is thirty-five and cannot read or write in English?

Sometimes these and many other challenges piled up so high around us that we felt completely overwhelmed and didn't know what to do. Yet the work we have *all* been called to as followers of Christ isn't always going to be easy, enjoyable, or entertaining. There are seasons that are immensely difficult and draining. Thomas Merton wrote in his book *New Seeds of Contemplation*, "God can always turn evil into good, though perhaps not always in a sense that would be understood by the preachers of sunshine and uplift." We lead ourselves astray when we think the Christian life is all about feel-good religiosity rather than the tough reality of loving others because we ourselves have been loved (1 John 4:19).

Consider this. Back in the first few centuries after Christ, there were frequent famines in the Roman Empire. Church writings from this period indicate that during such famines Christians would fast from their own meager supplies so that they might sustain their starving pagan neighbors. The early Christians took Paul literally when he instructed the church at Philippi, "In humility consider others better than yourselves. Each of you should look not only to your own interests, but also to the interests of others" (Philippians 2:3–4). Of course Paul was just building on Jesus' supreme example of selfless love—the Cross—as well as His instruction that the greatest commandments are "'Love the Lord your God with all your heart and with all your soul and with all your strength and with and all your mind'; and, 'Love your neighbor as yourself'" (Luke 10:27).

C. S. Lewis stated in *Mere Christianity,* "If our charities do not at all pinch or hamper us, I should say they are too small." Do we allow our love of others to "pinch or hamper us" today, or are we willing to love others only when it is convenient for us and not too demanding? In the United States alone, nearly two million people will face homelessness this next year. Around our world, more than a billion people are hungry. How many of us are willing to fast from *anything* (much less our own daily bread!) so that the poor around us might be cared for—fed, clothed, housed—in short, *loved?*

For most of us in the Western world, loving others probably doesn't mean that we need to stop eating. But I'm willing to bet that it *does* mean we can't go about our lives like our culture says we should—convinced that increasing our level of material wealth is the primary purpose of existence. Don't get me wrong: I don't know what good works God has for you to

223

do (Ephesians 2:8–10); that's your responsibility to discern day by day, moment by moment. But take heart. In the midst of the difficulty, frustration, confusion, and impossibility of trying to love others in Christ's name, hear the words of our Lord, who promised us that "whoever loses his life for my sake will find it" (Matthew 10:39).

Grace and peace to you as you seek to consider others as more significant than yourself. May you do so, not out of guilt, but rather because Christ did the same for you some two thousand years ago on top of a hill called Calvary.

Keep on.

MIKE YANKOSKI
Vancouver, B.C.
January 2010

A READER'S Q&A WITH MIKE

It's been several years since you and Sam have been on the streets. As you think back on your experience, do you think you would do it again?

If I could rewind my life, I would definitely do the whole journey again. Despite the difficulties Sam and I faced, I think the insight and understanding we gained couldn't have happened any other way. I learned so much about myself, about the American church, about the needs people on our city streets must face every day. The experience utterly changed me. Everything the Lord is leading me to do now—writing and speaking in the area of social justice, pursuing education with the hope of becoming a college professor, living in a community house that seeks to provide radical hospitality for those in need—is because of those five months on the street. Additionally, there will forever be a connection when I see someone who is homeless. I *know* (at least a little about) what it feels like to be there. I know now how much of a difference something as simple as a kind word, a cup of coffee, or a hot meal can make.

What would you say to others who might be considering a similar journey on the streets?

This is a delicate question, one that requires more time to answer well than I have here. I've written a much longer response, available at www.UnderTheOverpass.com/ThePlunge. That being said, here is a short version of the answer: Living on the streets is a unique way to gain a deeper understanding of what it's like to be homeless, but it is *not* the best way to serve and care for the people who are homeless. If you find yourself being led to care for the men and women who are on your city streets, a far more effective option than spending weeks or months on the streets would be to connect with a local organization or group of people and begin to address the practical and systemic issues faced by the homeless in your area. That way you'd be investing yourself in helping others address their needs, rather than spending all your time panhandling, trying to dry out after a rainstorm, or searching for a bathroom.

226

You and Sam lived on the streets for only five months. Do you think you were *really* "homeless"?

Sam and I *chose* to live on the streets, and that means we always knew our journey was going to end at some point. There was simply no way around this fact, and thus our experience of street life was fundamentally different from that of the men and women we were hanging out with every day. After all, most of them didn't know if they were ever going to get off the streets. Nevertheless, I do believe that Sam and I experienced a significant part of the reality that is homelessness. We had daily, pressing needs to attend to—hunger, thirst, danger, weather, and so on—that weren't impacted in the slightest by the fact that we would one day leave the streets. Though we certainly have no idea what it is like to be on the streets for years or decades, we did learn something about how hard even a single day can be. Thus I believe our journey on the streets and *Under the Overpass* (as the account of that journey) function like windows into (or paintings of, perhaps?) the reality which is homelessness. While our story certainly doesn't capture the full reality of life on the streets, hopefully it provides an accurate and unique view into a world most of us know little about.

Obviously you and Sam went through a lot of hard stuff while you were on the streets. If you could narrow it down to one thing, what would you say was the toughest aspect of living on the streets for those five months?

By far the hardest aspect was a lack of strong relationships. Of course we were always hanging out with one another, making new friends on the streets, and having conversations with other homeless people. Nevertheless, the streets can be a very lonely place, and we both felt that. And this was more than just mere homesickness or a longing for a warm, dry bed like the one I had slept on most of my life. I believe that we as humans are created for community, and therefore one of the most fundamental human needs is to be deeply known. The harsh reality for a person on the streets is that most people simply walk past and don't give you the time of day, while your friends within the homeless community may be gone the next week for any number of reasons. Though we were there for only five months, Sam and I felt this relational poverty strongly. Addressing this relational need is one of the

227

most difficult and essential aspects of caring for those on our streets.

As you look back on the experience you and Sam had on the streets, what is one thing that you wish you would have done differently?

One thing Sam and I have talked about is that we wish we had been more intentional in helping other homeless people get connected with the organizations in their area who might be able to help them. I think if we could do it over again, we would have spent more time trying to be a bridge between those local organizations and the people we were becoming friends with on the streets. This would have been difficult to do well, though, because we were in each city for only a few weeks.

Don't most homeless people *choose* to be there? If so, is it really possible to help people get off the streets?

I've met a lot of nonhomeless people who firmly believe that every homeless person chooses to be on the streets. They therefore think they don't need to care about or help them at all. "To each his own," they say to me with a look that means they fully expect me to agree with them. I fundamentally believe this is the wrong way to look at the situation. Where would I be (and where would *you* be) if God had simply said, "To each his own," and withheld His love? The good news of the gospel is that "while we were still sinners, Christ died for us" (Romans 5:8). It is this kind of love, undeserved and unconditional, that Christians are called to have for others, for we ourselves have been so loved.

Sam and I did meet a few people who said they "chose" to be there. But many of them, I am convinced, used "choice" as a coping mechanism to deal with the harsh reality of life on the streets. What I mean is this: They would say things like "I don't mind being here anymore," usually after telling us how many times they had tried to get off the streets, only to return again a while later. Because it's easier for humans to endure something if we feel like we *want* it, rather than if we feel like we're trapped in it, these men and women say they "choose" to be on the streets. But in any case, these people represented a tiny minority of the people we met. Most did not *choose* to be there but instead felt trapped and didn't know how to get off the streets.

This relates to the second part of the question. I absolutely do believe it is possible to help men and women transition off the streets. The obstacles many homeless people have—for example, mental illness, drug or alcohol addiction, and lack of education—can be overcome and are overcome every day. It must be said, though, that this is a long and involved process, one that most likely shouldn't be undertaken by lone individuals. It takes a lot of concentrated effort and a stable environment for people to overcome the things that have previously kept them on the streets.

Over the past few years I've done a lot of work with various rehabilitation programs and missions across North America that are connected with the Association of Gospel Rescue Missions (www.AGRM.org) From what I've seen, these organizations are the best way for men and women to transition off the streets. They provide long-term rehabilitation programs that are equipped with the necessary staff and knowledge to address the wide range of deep needs people on the streets have. Additionally, many offer education or job training programs that will help the person find a job once he or she graduates from the program.

In short, if you really want to help people get off the streets, one of the best things you can do is begin supporting and volunteering at your local rehabilitation center or rescue mission.

What is one memorable interaction you've had with a homeless person after you and Sam came back off the streets?

There have been many interactions with homeless people since Sam and I came back, but one stands out in particular. I was back in Portland, Oregon, about two years after Sam and I had been on the streets. (Despite looking, I wasn't able to locate anybody we'd been friends with during our time there.) I had a few extra hours and a few extra dollars, so I went to a small burrito stand and bought ten two-dollar bean-and-cheese burritos. I then spent the next few hours sitting down next to homeless people at some of Sam's and my old spots, offering them a burrito, and shooting the breeze with them. I asked questions like "Where are you from?" "How long have you been in Portland?" "What sports do you like?" Just trying to engage with them and treat them like human beings. It was broad daylight and I was in public areas with lots of other people in the vicinity, so I felt comfortable doing this alone.

One of the guys stopped chewing halfway through his burrito and looked straight at me. "Mike, do you realize you've changed my whole week?"

230

I stared at him in complete disbelief. Was the burrito *that* good? "What do you mean?"

I'll never forget his response: "You're the first person who has talked to me all week. Thank you."

I couldn't speak. Five minutes of my day and two dollars' worth of bean and cheese burrito changed someone's week!

Sometimes it's easy to walk by because we know we can't change someone's whole life in a single afternoon. But what we fail to realize is that simple kindness can go a long way toward encouraging someone who is stuck in a desolate place.

ACKNOWLEDGMENTS

O nly a fool journeys alone. I am humbled and blessed far beyond what I deserve by all those I've had the privilege to travel with in this life:

Sam Purvis—Without your willingness, faith and good company, this journey wouldn't have happened. Thanks for putting up with me, and for calling me on my crap! And thanks for enduring those months on the streets—hard but good.

Danae—Your letters, prayers, and love sustained me on the streets more than I can express. And now, what a gift it is to be married to you, my best friend! Wherever He leads us in this life, I am thankful to be journeying with you.

Mom and Dad—I'm still amazed that you allowed and supported this crazy idea, and I'm thankful. Who you are has forever shaped Fawn and me for the good. I love you both very much.

Fawn—I get the double blessing of having you as both my younger sister and my sister in Christ. You're a constant encouragement to me. I'm excited to live this life with you and Daniel!

Board of advisers—Thank you for leading, for praying, for investing, and for living as you do. You showed Sam and me the biblical truth that good advisers prepare the way for success. You are all men I hope and pray to become more like—maybe someday.

Parker (Colorado) Evangelical Presbyterian Church ("PEPC")—Thank you for being a living, active part of the worldwide body of Christ. The Lord is working through you to guide and strengthen many. Thanks for your prayers, encouragement, guidance, and support throughout this journey.

Sisters (Oregon) Community Church—Thank you for encouraging Sam to take this leap of faith with me. Your support and your encouragement along the way kept us going. Thank you for your willingness to sacrifice and serve around the world.

WaterBrook Multnomah—Thank you for your original vision for this book, and for your vision now to release this revised and updated edition. To Steve Cobb, president; to Ken Petersen, publisher; and to all the folks in marketing, sales, and editorial who have poured so many hours into this project—endless thanks. To my editor, David Kopp—it's has been a joy to work with you, then and now. Thank you for wrestling with the ideas and wordings with me, and for your commitment to helping me deliver the best reading experience possible. To two people in particular who have moved on in the years since the original release of *Under the Overpass:*

- Don Jacobson—Thank you for believing in this project from its earliest stages. Your support and encouragement along the way have meant more than you know. Glad we still get to hang out.
- Doug Gabbert—Your excitement and vision for

234

Under the Overpass were a real gift. Thanks for standing by Sam and me so many years ago. Keep on.

"The Boys"—You know who you are. Wherever you are in this world, live well and love much. Rejoice always. Thank you for letting me live this life alongside you, and for keeping me in line at so many points along the way.

You, the reader—Thank you for taking the time to journey with Sam and me. I hope and pray that you have been both challenged and encouraged along the way. May you ask the hard questions about your faith, your church, your life, your world. Count every moment of this life sacred, even as you are willing to lay it all down in pursuit of Christ.

235

WANT TO KNOW MORE?
...SOUND OFF?
...GET CONNECTED?

To find out more about our journey on the streets
or to share your thoughts about this book, go to:

UNDERTHEOVERPASS.COM

And, for an
in depth study/discussion guide
covering the new material in this edition,
go to:

UNDERTHEOVERPASS.COM/DISCUSSION

To inquire about having Mike speak at your church service, university event, or organizational gala, please visit

www.UnderTheOverpass.com/speaking

If you're passionate about helping others — but aren't sure where or how to focus your energy — *Zealous Love: A Practical Guide to Social Justice* offers information and ideas to help you integrate social justice into your life. Mike & Danae Yankoski's new book introduces you to eight of the world's most pressing challenges: hunger, unclean water, HIV/AIDS, creation degradation, lack of education, economic inequality, refugees, and human trafficking. But it does more than educate. It provides real, practical, do-able steps anyone can take to help make a difference. Through first-hand accounts and up-to-date facts about these eight global issues, *Zealous Love* provides readers with the information, inspiration, and ideas they need to make a difference in their world.

Check out www.ZealousLove.org
for more information or visit your favorite bookstore.